Indigenous Archaeology

Indigenous Archaeology

American Indian Values and Scientific Practice

Joe Watkins

ALTAMIRA
P R E S S

A Division of
ROWMAN & LITTLEFIELD PUBLISHERS, INC.
Walnut Creek • Lanham • New York • Oxford

ALTA MIRA PRESS
A Division of Rowman & Littlefield Publishers, Inc.
1630 North Main Street, #367
Walnut Creek, CA 94596
http://www.altamirapress.com

Rowman & Littlefield Publishers, Inc.
4720 Boston Way
Lanham, MD 20706

12 Hid's Copse Road
Cumnor Hill, Oxford OX2 9JJ, England

British Library Cataloguing in Publication Information Available

Library of Congress Cataloging-in-Publication Data

Watkins, Joe, 1951–
    Indigenous archaeology : American Indian values and scientific practice / Joe
Watkins.
        p.   cm.
    Includes bibliographical references and index.
    ISBN 0-7425-0328-3 (cloth : alk. paper) — ISBN 0-7425-0329-1 (pbk. : alk.
paper)
        1. Indians of North America—Antiquities—Collection and preservation.
2. Archaeology—United States.   3. Cultural property—Repatriation—United
States.   4. Human remains (Archaeology)—United States.
5. Anthropological ethics—United States.   I. Title.

E77.9 .W37   2000
973.1—dc21   00-044802

Printed in the United States of America

⊚™ The paper used in this publication meets the minimum requirements of
American National Standard for Information Sciences—Permanence of
Paper for Printed Library Materials, ANSI/NISO Z39.48-1992.

Contents

Acknowledgments

The writing of this book has not been a one person job. Without the help of all those involved, it never would have reached completion.

First, I wish to acknowledge the help and support of my wife and family who understood when I wrung my hands over unanticipated delays in getting the chapter drafts finished.

I also wish to acknowledge the help of friends and colleagues: to Marjy Duncan who read through my dissertation and offered insightful comments regarding its strengths and weaknesses; to Richard Wilk and Anne Pyburn who convinced me that publishing this book was a good idea; to the reviewers—Stayce Hathorn, Matthew Purtill, David Hurst Thomas, and Edward C. Brodnicki—who helped make this a better volume, and especially to Mitch Allen, who helped bring this entire process to fruition.

Much of this book has been taken from my original dissertation research, and the acknowledgments made in that work should be restated here. Without the inspiration of Dr. Robert E. Bell who told me to do what I liked doing before retiring instead of waiting until after; the help of Dr. Jack Hofman for helping me get started again; the support of Dr. Robert Brooks, Oklahoma State archaeologist, for obtaining funding for the copying and mailing costs of the questionnaire; the conversations and arguments with John Hartley that stimulated the research; and the members of my dissertation committee, who waded through the rough drafts and helped me write what I hoped to say, none of this would have ever been written.

And, of course, I must also acknowledge my mother, who instilled in me the desire for education and the need to learn.

O～O⋈O～O

Introduction

Why don't more American Indians get involved in archaeology? I'm not sure there is an answer to that question—at least not an easy one.

Perhaps a story will help. I was walking across Cambridge Common, trying to find my way to the Peabody Museum. I must have looked a little lost (as I was) and perhaps broke an unwritten rule by walking across the grass. As I passed an elderly woman sitting on a park bench, feeding popcorn to a flock of pigeons, I heard her say "Stupid foreigners," not quite under her breath, but fairly close to it.

I slowed and turned, curious about whom she was speaking, and saw a look of distaste in her eyes that rocked me a bit. Only then did I realize she was talking about me. I stopped only for a moment, and then smiled at the irony of it all.

My ancestors on my father's side have been on this continent for perhaps 15,000 years, give or take a few hundred years, while her's, giving her the full benefit of the doubt considering her dress and appearance, 380 years at the most. Maybe I don't belong at Harvard, but who is the true foreigner?

American Indians often feel they are the foreigners in the Land of Prehistory, to steal a title from Alice Beck Kehoe (1998). Their passports, wrought from their bloodlines and their culture, are carefully scrutinized each time they cross the borders, and even when they become "naturalized citizens" of the Land, their passports seem to bear the words "Watch out for this one!" They feel uncomfortable at the border crossings between their land and the foreign land, uncomfortable with a seemingly "Jekyll and Hyde" existence, with neither set of citizenry able to recognize its true character.

In my first years in archaeology, I was taught that science was first and foremost an unbiased attempt at compartmentalizing the natural world, that archaeology was the only option available to "write" the unrecorded history of American Indians, and that archaeological resources were the "pages" of the book of history.

My grandmother instilled in me my desire to help maintain the history of the American Indian. When I found an Archaic projectile point at my family homestead and showed it to her, she told me (through my cousin who translated) that it was part of the history of those who had lived there before the Choctaw were moved to Oklahoma, and that it was important not to forget that history.

Later, however, I was shown another side of what has become a multifaceted issue, that the scientific method might also be considered to be only a thinly disguised way of separating archaeologists from other grave desecrators.

I first encountered such an opinion concerning my choice of careers in 1973, when, after being introduced as an archaeologist to a Comanche Indian man, I was asked if I was one of those "bone diggers." I answered that I had never excavated human remains, didn't want to, and never would, but such an explanation was insufficient. Leroy Mason would not believe me then, and probably, if he is still alive today, would still consider me "one of those."

The exact beginning of the conflict between American Indians and anthropologists may never be determined, but anthropologists tie its origins within the early development of American anthropology in the United States. American Indian authors, such as Vine Deloria Jr. (1969), Jack F. Trope and Walter Echo-Hawk (1992), and James Riding In (1992), however, tie its history to the gruesome collections made by battlefield medics of the U.S. Army Surgeon's office and to anthropologists on late-night grave-robbing expeditions. Anthropologists claimed to be saving the information for science and the Indians themselves, while the Indians claimed they were tired of being treated only as bits and pieces of information to be saved. Few members of either side appeared to recognize the rights of the other side. Regardless of who recounts this history, it is one filled with distrust and innuendo.

The 1969 publication of Deloria's *Custer Died for Your Sins* brought discussion of the conflict into mainstream America, and scientists began to see the need for cooperation. Individual archaeologists such as Elden Johnson (1973) and Roderick Sprague (1974) called for the development of working relationships with American Indian groups, but, in general, the profession of archaeology seemed to remain distant from those whose ancestors they studied.

Which brings us to the title of this book. In 1996, I was asked to teach American Indian tribal members an introductory class on archaeology. Rather than teach the same course I would have taught to incoming college freshmen, I chose to orient the class toward an American Indian perspective, focusing on ideas and techniques of most use to the tribes. This has been my choice through the development of this manuscript, to focus on issues that I see as being of most interest to American Indians as they relate to the conflict that has developed between American Indians and archaeologists in the past. Other researchers would likely have chosen other issues; I hope others soon will.

The current research involves a more detailed examination of the underlying causes of this conflict. If American Indian disruptions of archaeological excavations and museum displays in the 1970s were merely politically motivated, then archaeologists' reactions could be better understood. If, however, those actions could be attributed to concerns based in American Indian cultural values, then archaeologists should focus their attention on developing better relationships with these cultural groups.

This study focuses primarily on what I term "compliance" archaeology (cultural resource management) and its legislated background rather than on "academic" archaeology, which has more latitude in dealing with problems. Those archaeologists who practice compliance archaeology are more regulated by federal laws and procedures in the practice of the craft, whereas private or academic ("pure research" oriented) archaeologists have fewer constraints placed on them regarding a project.

Repatriation legislation such as the National Museum of the American Indian Act and the Native American Graves Protection and Repatriation Act have also codified choices that were once voluntary—essentially legislating a great number of archaeologists' professional ethics. Legislation has been enacted that forces consultation with affected American Indian groups, thereby removing the opportunity for individuals to make an ethical choice rather than simply following the letter of the law. In spite of the legislation, however, it is still possible for an individual to circumvent the intent of the law by consulting solely with the factions of a tribe known to be sympathetic or supportive of the individual, for example, or to play the elected officials against the traditional leaders (or vice versa).

It is, therefore, this "gray area," where ethics are legislated yet open to manipulation, that is the focus of this research. When one examines the rhetoric spewed forth by both sides in the newspaper dispatches relating to Kennewick, it is surprising how differently the law that led to the current impasse is interpreted. But it is when one hears concerned archaeologists or American Indians each moaning about the undermining of their rights relative to cultural resources or human remains that the importance of research such as this is realized.

This book is presented in two parts. Part I (chapters 1–5) provides an outline of the situation between American Indians and archaeologists as it exists today. Chapters 1 and 2 focus on the history of the conflict between American Indians and archaeologists and present a brief history of ethics and the growth of professionalism in anthropology and archaeology. The statements on ethics issued by various archaeological societies generally carry with them implied consent of their membership even though adherence is not required.

Chapter 3 provides a general presentation of various pieces of legislation that form the base for compliance archaeology (cultural resource management) within the United States, while chapter 4 more closely examines repatriation legislation (the National Museum of the American Indian Act and the Native American Graves Protection and Repatriation Act) and its impact on anthropology.

Chapter 5 presents the results of research aimed at gaining an understanding of the factors that most influence the attitudes of American archaeologists in their decisions on conducting archaeological research.

Part II (chapters 6–10) provides case studies to illustrate some of the problems discussed in part I. Chapter 6 examines the development of the Navajo Tribe in cultural resources management and the tribe's relationship to the practice of archaeology. Chapter 7 examines the situation in Kansas and Nebraska between the Pawnee Tribe and the historical societies concerning the closure of a tourist "attraction" that displayed pre-contact American Indian human remains. Chapters 8 and 9 recount two situations in the state of Washington where American Indian involvement with the discipline exceeded the normal relationship and echoed the protests of the 1970s: the East Wenatchee Clovis Cache and the Kennewick discovery.

Chapter 10 provides a glimpse into the status of the relations between anthropologists and indigenous populations in other industrialized countries as a means of putting the current situation in the United States in a more worldwide framework.

The final chapter summarizes the issues discussed and provides suggestions for the development of an indigenous archaeology— archaeology as a discipline developed with the control and influence of indigenous populations around the world.

It is hoped that this book will provide the reader and the archaeologist with a glimpse of the reality of research at the end of the twentieth century. The colonial attitudes of archaeology as a social science have been brought to light numerous times by numerous authors, but few methodological changes have been observed over the years. Repatriation legislation has forced archaeologists to reexamine their ties and relationships with indigenous populations, and individual archaeologists have made great strides in involving American Indians in their research (see Dongoske, Aldenderfer, and Doehner 2000), but the discipline *as a whole* has made only a few halting steps at alleviating the situation.

This research demonstrates that archaeology can learn from studies focused inward, that self-examination is important for growth, and that the populations it studies can indeed offer insights that will make the discipline stronger and more relevant to everyone.

Part I

o~oⵔⵔo~o

Issues

In the fall of 1990, I became interested in the conflict between American Indian groups and archaeologists following the discovery and excavation of large Clovis points (the East Wenatchee Clovis Cache) near East Wenatchee, Washington. That study, detailed in chapter 8, formed the pivot point for my dissertation and urged me to examine the historical and philosophical foundations of archaeology's relationships with American Indians.

Before I began my research, I viewed archaeology as a rather benign science. I had read Bruce Trigger (1980, 1986, 1989) and agreed with many of his ideas, but mostly I wondered whether archaeologists were as biased as Trigger thought them to be, or whether they were just well-meaning bumblers who sometimes heavy-handedly disturbed and fractured fragile relationships. I became intrigued and, in 1991, initiated a research project aimed at quantifying archaeolgists' attitudes toward American Indian issues. With the 1992 publication of Randall H. McGuire's paper on archaeology and its relationships with American Indians (1992a), it became apparent that other archaeologists were also trying to understand the paths that led American archaeology to its current relationship with American Indians.

At roughly the same time, the Society for American Archaeology began examining its relationships with the various "publics" with which it interacted, including American Indians and other indigenous populations. While ethics are considered to be the moral choices that govern the actions of an individual or a profession, most archaeologists involved in public archaeology or cultural resource management rely more heavily on procedures established through federal legislation to guide their interactions with indigenous populations on cultural issues.

Additionally, the passage of repatriation legislation in 1989 and 1990 greatly influenced my research. American Indian struggles to repatriate human remains, grave goods, and sacred artifacts from museum and federal collections impacted not only archaeology's relationships with indigenous populations but also moved that conflict out of the academic tower and into a more public forum—the U.S. Congress. And with that movement into the public view, archaeologists became more aware of American Indian perceptions of their discipline.

Thus, three major factors came together at the beginning of the 1990s that influenced archaeology's relationship with American Indians—one archaeological, one philosophical, and one legal. The decade that followed was one of questioning and posturing, with both American Indians and archaeologists trying to find a way to come to terms with the changes those outside influences wrought on the discipline.

The following chapters place the historical, philosophical, and legal basis of archaeology's relationship with American Indians—the veritable skeleton upon which the discipline's relationships are built—into perspective. They also provide the reader with a common starting place from which to examine American Indian approaches to controlling the cultural resources of their homelands.

1

o~o▷◁o~o

American Indians
and Archaeologists:
A Stormy Relationship

Into each life, it is said, some rain must fall, some people have
bad horoscopes, others take tips on the stock market, but Indians have been cursed above all other people in history. Indians
have anthropologists. (Deloria 1969: 78)

Perhaps it is only coincidental that, until the 1969 publication of
Vine Deloria Jr.'s book, *Custer Died for Your Sins*, American Indians shared an uneasy truce with anthropology and its subdiscipline of archaeology. Very little appeared, at least in print, that could
be interpreted as an opening salvo in a battle over control of culture or cultural artifacts. But, with the printing of excerpts of *Custer*
in *Playboy* magazine in August 1969, the nonacademic world was
made aware of American Indian distrust and discontent with the
discipline.

Maybe the social and political unrest of the times spurred American Indians to action, but American Indian protests for the period
1969–1979 (Watkins 1994, appendix B) showed that their distrust of
archaeology and archaeologists revolved primarily around the perceived threat to their ancestors and human remains. The general
attitudes of the more radical Indians in the 1970s were easily recognized by articles such as "Indian Skeleton" (Anonymous 1970:
12); "Don't Exploit Our Dead or Our Ceremonies or Our Dances"
(Anonymous 1971: 10); and "Archaeologists and the Indians" (Hall

1971: 10). Political groups organized to stop or disrupt excavation of prehistoric archaeological sites and cemeteries, as exemplified by the American Indian Movement's disruption of excavations at Welch, Minnesota, in 1971. They organized protests such as the occupation of the Southwest Museum in Los Angeles in 1971 in an attempt to get American Indian human remains and sensitive material out of public displays. And tribal groups began addressing the desire for the repatriation of human remains and artifacts with the fight for the return of the Onondaga wampum belts in 1969 from the State Museum of New York.

A BRIEF HISTORY LESSON

A number of anthropologists (see Bettinger 1991; Downer 1997; Ferguson 1996; Kehoe 1998; Lurie 1988; McGuire 1992a, 1992b, 1997; Meltzer 1983; Trigger 1980, 1986, 1989) have traced the history of anthropology and its relationship with American Indians, and an in-depth analysis is neither warranted nor attempted here. Suffice it to say that a growing body of evidence, as epitomized by Bruce Trigger's works, indicates that science does not operate in a vacuum from the social structure in which it occurs. Trigger's analysis—based primarily on the assumption that American colonialistic attitudes have influenced not only the manner in which the government has treated the American Indian but also the way that anthropologists have studied and portrayed them—is that "problems social scientists choose to research and (hopefully less often) the conclusions that they reach are influenced in various ways . . . (among them) . . . the attitudes and opinions that are prevalent in the societies in which they live" (1980: 662).

He goes on to argue that during the first half of America's existence (1770s through the 1870s), American Indians were held to be inferior to civilized men in order to rationalize the seizure of Indian lands, and that, eventually, racial myths grew to supplant any other myths about the Indians as a justification for waging war on the Indians and violating their treaty rights.

An example of the scientific treatment of American Indian development revolved around what Gordon R. Willey and Jeremy Sabloff (1980: 35) have called the "Mound Builder controversy." Those readers who have studied archaeology are aware of the Mound Builders and their place within the history of America, but, for the uninitiated, they provide an excellent example of the treatment of American Indians by archaeology.

The Mound Builders were believed to have been a non-Indian race, perhaps related to the prehistoric Mexicans, who had withdrawn from eastern North America or had been exterminated by the newly arrived Indians. Most writers of the period felt that these Mound Builders had constructed the enormous mounds because it was felt that the Indians of North America were not capable of such feats of engineering. Two notable exceptions to this school of thought were Samuel F. Haven (1856) and Henry R. Schoolcraft (1854), contemporary "archaeologists" who opposed the "Mound Builder as separate race" hypothesis.

But the controversy was not only a scholarly debate. As Donald D. Fowler Jr. noted, "The Myth of the Moundbuilders was never official government policy, but it did bolster arguments for moving the 'savage' Indians out of the way of white 'civilization'" (1987: 230). The extermination of American Indians by westward moving settlements of the United States was made morally easier by the apparent primitiveness of the natives, and the controversy served well as a justification for exterminating the Indian groups that had destroyed North America's only "civilized" culture (Trigger 1980: 665; Willey and Sabloff 1980; 40). Robert Bettinger agrees, stating "[m]uch simplified, Indians were savages . . . Americans were civilized . . . The philosophy of social evolutionary progress assured Americans it was their manifest destiny to civilize the New World, to replace savagery with civilization" (1991: 32–33).

Randall H. McGuire argues that the Mound Builder myth also worked to remove the Indian's ancestors from the history of the United States: "By routing the red savages, the new, civilized, White American race inherited the mantle, the heritage, of the old civilization" (1992a: 820). By the time archaeologists finally proved the mounds were products of the ancestors of the Indians who were encountered by the first colonists and westward travelers, the Indians mostly had been dispossessed of their land.

Yet, the demolition of the lost Mound Builder race hypothesis by Cyrus Thomas of the Bureau of Ethnology (later Bureau of American Ethnology) of the Smithsonian Institution in 1894 (Willey and Sabloff 1980: 43) and Fredrick Ward Putnam of the Peabody

Museum did nothing to change the popular attitudes against the American Indian.

In a more critical history of the discipline of archaeology, Alice Beck Kehoe (1998) argues that archaeology continues to treat American Indians as belonging outside of science, and that scientists act as if only they have the ability to understand the processes that led to the development of American Indian culture and prehistory.

While the Mound Builder controversy might serve as an example of archaeology's concerns with American Indian issues, the unrest of the 1970s was much more personal. Even though there were no organized protests in the southern Great Plains against archaeology, the widespread circulation of American Indian newspapers and journals did have its influence. I recall struggling to come to terms with the American Indian Movement (AIM) disruptions and the Onondaga fight for their cultural patrimony. As an archaeologist-in-training, as it were, I believed that archaeology was one of the better methods of gaining an understanding of the "unrecorded" history in the ground, and that the safest place for artifacts of importance to tribes was in museums. But I also felt a bit betrayed that museums and archaeologists could not understand why American Indian desires had to be taken more seriously. I recall professors who seemingly dismissed the protesters with an "if they only knew what we really do, they'd appreciate us more" attitude (perhaps suggesting that only the uneducated were concerned about such things).

A few archaeology professors laughed at cartoons where American Indians proposed to excavate Arlington National Cemetery, but most chose to ignore them. They were not "grave robbers" but scientists; unfortunately, they were not interested in explaining to the public what they did and lost an opportunity to alleviate the situation as it was growing.

While American Indian protesters worked outside the system to try to influence change, other groups worked within it to try to protect their cultural materials.

AMERICAN INDIANS AND HISTORIC PRESERVATION

A brief review of the historic preservation movement in the United States (Hosmer 1965, 1981; King 1999; King, Hickman, and Berg

1977; Smith and Ehrenhard 1991) makes it clear that early historic preservation efforts were based primarily on upper-class values applied to Euroamerican concepts of history practiced by nationalist-focused groups.

Perhaps Trigger's implication that anthropology has become the study of allegedly simpler people, while history has become the study of groups that have evolved into civilizations (1986: 89), is also implicit in the term "historic preservation," since it seems to focus on saving those things whose purpose was fulfilled primarily in the past. For example, Roger Anyon discusses the evolution of the pueblo of Zuni into "a modern town atop a complex archaeological site" (1991: 218). Often, tourists visit Zuni expecting to see a cramped, dusty, five-story structure that Americans have come to know as a pueblo. They are often disappointed, however, when they encounter not a dusty pueblo but a series of one-story structures surrounded by suburbs.

Yet, in spite of this Euroamerican focus, American Indians began applying historic preservation ideas to their culture. In January 1972, the Navajo Tribal Council passed a resolution enacting an antiquities preservation law for the Navajo Reservation. This resolution acknowledged the existence of the many ruins and artifacts on the reservation, and the fact that the sites and objects were irreplaceable and invaluable in the study of the history and preservation of the cultural background of the Navajo Nation. It went on to set up procedures for permitting archaeological studies, punishing law breakers, and protecting the resources. This resolution was one of the first attempts to extend tribal protection over cultural resources on tribal lands. Given the 1971 disruptions of the Welch, Minnesota, archaeological excavations and the takeover of a Colorado State University anthropology laboratory by AIM members, this action was apparently in contrast to the more radical view of archaeology as counterproductive to American Indian wishes.

Later that same year, in the fall of 1972, Thomas F. King of the Advisory Council on Historic Preservation, authored an article that outlined "Archaeological Law and the American Indian." He discussed four classes of laws that he felt would deal with American Indians and the protection of their cultural heritage and also provided model policies for the protection of tribal resources. In this manner, he hoped to protect the cultural remains that were being lost: "For every skeleton that has reached the security—if not dignity—of an anthropological storage room, easily ten thousand have been ground under bulldozers, floated away under reservoirs, or ended up with their skulls grinning on mantelpieces as candle-holders or bookends" (1972: 31).

King's suggestions made sense if the tribes wanted to "protect" their cultural material from destruction by vandals or heavy equip-ment, but it also played on the fears of American Indians by graphi-cally reinforcing the idea that there were people (obviously not ar-chaeologists!) who would go so far as to use skulls as decorator items. And, by noting the "security—if not dignity—of an anthro-pological storage room," King reinforced the archaeologist's belief that we were "saving" these materials. But who were we saving them for?

In 1974, two attorneys examined the relationship between historic preservation, as an action, and the American Indian. In an article entitled "What is America's Heritage? Historic Preservation and American Indian Culture," Paul E. Wilson and Elaine Oser Zingg discussed how the traditional implication of historic preservation ("the protection of a tangible thing") had to be altered so that the American Indian could give special attention to the "preservation of natural areas where he lived and worshiped and to the subter-ranean remains of his ancestral communities and the historic burial grounds of his people" (1974: 418).

They closed with a statement that all scientists involved with the study of the American Indian should heed: "One of the tasks of the law of historic preservation is to maintain an environment in which it is possible for Indians to remain Indians and for other Americans to know and appreciate and respect them as Indians and Ameri-cans" (1974: 452).

But could Indians remain Indians and continue to work within the system? In 1974, toward the end of my first year of graduate school, I was told by a professor that the only reason I got accepted into graduate school was because I was Indian and because I had my own funding. What made it important for him to differentiate me from the other students, a distaste for a perceived "equal op-portunity admission"? I fought to find a way where I could work in archaeology and not have to confront the conflict. I originally chose to focus on Old World prehistory ("to go over there and dig up *their* ancestors"), but was not able to pursue that course. I eventually chose "experimental archaeology," thereby by-passing humans altogether and focusing instead on the tools and technology they created.

But still I was not able to escape the problem. I carried a double-edged curse—archaeologists did not think I could be an "objective" scientist and American Indians distrusted my motives. As a "Native American specialist/archaeologist" for the Atlanta office of the Interagency Archaeological Services/Heritage Conservation and Recreation Services, I thought I might be able to influence both archaeologists and American Indians by confronting issues that American Indians faced in regard to archaeology rather than turning a blind eye to them. I tried to get American Indian input on issues at the federal level through pointed questions during the American Indian Religious Freedom Act consultations held in 1978.

But while a few archaeologists may have been confronting the issue, analysis of the conflict was more often undertaken by individuals from other fields. In 1982, attorney Dean B. Suagee, in "American Indian Religious Freedom and Cultural Resources Management: Protecting Mother Earth's Caretakers," followed a similar viewpoint espoused by Wilson and Zingg ten years earlier. Suggesting that American Indians, by the very nature of their concern for the natural world, cannot separate "cultural" resources from "natural" ones, Suagee discussed the legal issues of the sanctity of science versus the sanctity of the grave. Eventually, he states "the earlier in planning that Indian religious concerns are brought forward, the more likely it is that alternative sites or projects will be given serious consideration" (1982: 54). Even Suagee seemed predisposed to believe that archaeology would grind on, regardless of tribal concerns, and that it was up to the tribe to get their concerns in early or lose out.

But the special nature of American Indian historic preservation concerns was being noted. A 1990 article by two anthropologists explored the manner in which American Indian groups approach the task of deciding which resources of an indivisible continuum to be protected, and which could be allowed to be impacted. In "Holistic Conservation and Cultural Triage: American Indian Perspectives on Cultural Resources," Richard W. Stoffle and Michael J. Evans outline the shift from "holistic conservation" (total protection) to "cultural triage," where "a forced choice situation in which an ethnic group [is] faced with the decision to rank in importance cultural resources that could be impacted by a proposed development project" (1990: 95).

Today, more tribal groups are adapting archaeological practices and methodology to protect cultural resources on their reservations. In fact, as a result of the 1992 amendments to the National Historic Preservation Act, twelve American Indian tribes took over a portion of the historic preservation duties from state historic preservation officers in July 1996 (National Park Service 1996), and, as of February 1999, seventeen tribes had tribal historic preservation officers in place to formally participate in the national historic preservation program. The historic preservation program of the Navajo Nation is discussed in more detail in chapter 6, but another example will illustrate this point.

Following the Mexican–American War, army columns crossing the American Southwest encountered numerous large ruins. Not believing that the existing American Indian groups of the area could have been capable of constructing such structures, the discoverers credited their construction to the civilizations of Mesoamerica, giving them names such as "Montezuma's Castle" and "Aztec Ruins." This implied that the Pueblos were only imitators of the lost race that had created the ruins (McGuire 1992a: 821), rather than the actual descendants of those who had built them.

In spite of this attitude, the Zuni Tribe of New Mexico has been involved in cultural preservation programs since the formal establishment of the Zuni Archaeology Program in 1978 (Anyon and Ferguson 1995; Mills and Ferguson 1998). The tribe has been able to protect its cultural resources in the manner it wishes, without relying on outsiders to implement alien policies and procedures. The policies of the Pueblo of Zuni regarding cultural resources management was set out in a series of seven tribal council resolutions that "affirm the need for and benefits of cultural resource management, and outline the active role the Pueblo of Zuni wants to play in the federal cultural resources management compliance process" (Mills and Ferguson 1998: 32).

Additionally, the 1991 formulation of the Cultural Resources Advisory Team of the Pueblo of Zuni added another process by which cultural resources might be protected by the pueblo. Barbara

J. Mills and T. J. Ferguson note that the "Zuni Tribe is fortunate to have its own ongoing archaeological program because it provides an interface between the historic preservation bureaucracy and the tribal structure" (1998: 40) in such a way to alleviate the conflict between the tribe and outside interests.

THE EXCAVATION AND REBURIAL OF HUMAN REMAINS

In 1973, Elden Johnson listed the excavation of burials first among four recurrent themes of protests by American Indians (Johnson 1973: 129). The article ended with the hope that those themes "be dealt with collectively by responsible members of a professional society and that the issues will not continue to be met post hoc by individuals and single institutions as reactions to protests" (130).

Most tribal groups do not wish graves to be excavated, and are generally united in their views to have the human remains that have been excavated returned to the tribes. Recall that the protests and occupation of the Southwest Museum in Los Angeles in 1971 were aimed at calling public attention to the issue in order to get skeletal material removed from display and reburied. The interests of American Indians were not being ignored at the national level by archaeologists, even though there were no organized national programs to integrate their concerns.

In 1974, the National Park Service awarded a grant to the Society for American Archaeology (SAA) to fund a series of "Six Seminars on the Future Direction of Archaeology" (McGimsey and Davis 1977). One of these seminars, "Archaeology and Native Americans," was proposed to review the relationship between archaeologists and American Indians and to "alleviate misunderstanding, to increase communication, to sensitize archaeologists to Native American concerns, and to sensitize Native Americans to the capability of archaeology to contribute to an understanding of the heritage we have all gained from Native American cultures" (90). This was one of the first attempts to "institutionalize" the approach of archaeologists to the conflict between them and American Indians, and it is interesting to note that the framers of the seminars considered American Indian concerns to be one of the six major issues facing the discipline at that time.

In 1978, Congress passed Public Law 95-341, the American Indian Religious Freedom Act, a resolution that called for "the United States to protect and preserve for American Indians their inherent right of freedom to believe, express, and exercise the traditional religions . . . including but not limited to access to sites, use and possession of sacred objects and the freedom to worship through ceremonials and traditional rites." Section 2 of the act called for the "various Federal departments . . . responsible for administering relevant laws to evaluate their policies and procedures in consultation with native traditional religious leaders in order to determine appropriate changes necessary to protect and preserve Native American religious cultural rights and practices."

A series of ten consultations with American Indian groups were held throughout the United States in 1979 to obtain input about the various federal agencies' regulations. A report was issued in August 1979 in fulfillment of the law. Concerns listed by American Indian groups at these consultations centered around various general areas, but of relevance to archaeology were concerns about access to and protection of cemeteries, burials, and sacred objects (primarily those in museum collections).

During the late 1970s, various federal agencies had "in house" policies concerning human remains. Within the Department of the Interior, the Heritage Conservation and Resource Services (HCRS) maintained a "Policy on Disposition of Human Remains" that served as a model for most other federal agencies involved with archaeological human skeletal material. The policy called for reburial of skeletal materials recovered from marked or identified deliberate interments when direct kinship to individuals could be demonstrated and also where a "demonstrable ethnic affinity to specific living groups of Native Americans or others" could be established, but only after "appropriate documentation and study are completed" (Heritage Conservation and Resource Services 1978). Those human remains that could not be identified to a specific contemporary ethnic group were to be maintained within collections.

I pointed out to Forrest Gerard, the assistant secretary of the Department of the Interior at the time, that the policy was thought to be "fair" since it allowed for the scientific study of human materials while at the same time allowing reburial following the wishes of lineal descendants or those who could demonstrate an ethnic affinity to the remains.

However, T. J. Ferguson, a tribal archaeologist in the Zuni Archaeology Program, commented on the policy and pointed out that "foremost among the shortcomings is a bias in the policy towards the belief system of the dominant Euro-american culture" (1979: 1). He hoped the policy could be restructured "so that it makes Indian values and beliefs as important in policy matters as those of archaeologists" (3).

Changes to the policy were suggested in 1980, making it more open to American Indian wishes. It called for "contact [with] those ethnic groups which are most probably related to the archaeological group as determined or suggested by geographical, historical, or anthropological data" (Watkins 1980: 1) prior to archaeological investigations that might impact human skeletal remains. A one-year time limit was proposed for the analysis of those materials for which no direct ancestors could be identified, followed by a ten-year limit on the curation of the material before reburial of the remains. It also proposed a set of procedures in the eventuality that human remains were discovered as a result of natural or mechanically induced processes.

The proposed revisions were seen as a step in the right direction by requiring consultation with affected groups, time limits during which the materials could be analyzed and curated, a system that allowed for reburial, and a set of procedures for "inadvertent discovery" situations. In spite of the suggestions (or, perhaps, because of them), federal agencies were slow to change the policy. In retrospect, it is surprising to me how many of these "suggestions" might be seen as precursors to some portions of recent repatriation and reburial legislation.

A short time later, in 1982, attorney Dean Higginbotham examined the legal issues inherent in the conflict between the viewpoints of the American Indian and archaeologists. In "Native Americans versus Archaeologists: The Legal Issues," he discusses the sorts of issues likely to arise in cases where archaeologists and traditional Indians take uncompromising stances concerning "the excavation of historic and prehistoric skeletal remains of Native Americans and artifactual materials of religious significance" (1982: 91). He also provided an analysis of certain rights of American Indians under state and federal statutes as they existed in the early 1980s.

American Indian concerns with archaeology were becoming more visible to archaeologists. The 1985 conference on reburial issues,

held in Chicago at the Newberry Library's Darcy McNickle Center
for the History of the American Indian, brought together twenty-
three participants representing a range of interest groups—
academic and administrative archaeologists; American Indian
spiritual, tribal, and political leaders; physical and cultural anthropologists; lawyers; museum administrators; and historians. Discussions centered around five major topics:

1. reasons for insisting upon reburial,
2. reasons for objecting to reburial,
3. reasons for scientific study of human skeletal populations,
4. exploration of possible resolutions, and
5. the next step. (Dincauze 1985: 1)

A report containing the transcripts of the meeting published by
the SAA provided a "Consensus of the Reburial Conference": the
necessity for respect for human remains (No. 1), the need for public education (No. 4), the need to protect materials from vandalism,
looting, and desecration (No. 5), and the need for cooperation between anthropologists and American Indians (Nos. 2, 4, and 6)
(Quick 1985: 175). Statement No. 7 called for materials such as "a
statement on the ethics pertaining to excavation and reburial; possible changes to ARPA, NHPA, appropriate federal laws and regulations, model state level legislation (nonprescriptive); and . . . the
matter of deaccession" (175).

The following year, on April 24, 1986, the SAA held a plenary
session at the 51st annual meeting of the Society on the Treatment
of Human Remains. Their goal was to "refine a series of principles
for ethical and socially responsible actions in situations involving
the excavation, analysis, curation and ultimate disposition of human remains by archaeologists" (Watson 1986: 1). This session resulted in the issuance of a "Statement Concerning the Treatment of
Human Remains" in May 1986 (Society for American Archaeology
1986). This statement, rather than simplifying the issue, may have
done the opposite.

It called for the concerns of different cultures to be channeled
through "designated representatives and leaders"; stated that all
human remains should receive appropriate scientific study; opposed universal or indiscriminate reburial of human remains; and
opposed any federal legislation seeking to impose a uniform stan-

dard for determining the disposition of all human remains.

In response to this statement, the National Congress of American Indians in 1986 adopted two resolutions that dealt with the treatment of human remains exhumed by archaeologists. The first resolution condemned the U.S. Department of the Interior's policy regarding the disposition of human remains and recommended litigation to invalidate the policy. The second resolution supported "the efforts of Indian and Native governments and organizations to reclaim and protect their national treasures and cultural patrimony" (Society of Professional Archaelogists 1986: 3).

In April 1987, the Society of Professional Archaeologists (SOPA) introduced a proposed reburial policy that dealt with ethical and legal considerations in the treatment of human remains (Niquette 1987: 1). The proposed policy would have affected those remains with at least fifty years of elapsed time following their interment. It also called for exhumation when relocation or protection is not feasible; no exhumation of human remains for research or training purposes if they are not in danger; balancing cultural and religious importance with their significance in contemporary and predictable future research; consultation with biological or culturally related groups of the deceased, including tribes currently or previously occupying the land in which the deceased lay; nonreinterment of human remains and related artifacts until their research significance has been exhausted (including for perpetuity and subjection of the materials to analyses that partially destroys or modifies them); reinterment of human remains of lesser significance in accordance with state or local law and/or the wishes of biological or cultural descendants (or tribal groups who occupy or previously occupied the lands in which the deceased lay); and, finally, reinterment of human remains and grave associated artifacts "having demonstrated cultural or religious significance of such magnitude that their analysis would impose an unconstitutional burden on the free exercise of religion by their descendants" (Niquette 1987: 2).

In October 1987, the editor of the SOPA newsletter presented responses to this proposed policy (Gummerman 1987: 2). Various suggestions were made for addition to the proposed policy ("curation in the ground—reburial after initial study has been exhausted") and deletion from the policy ("reburial . . . only where there is a clear and demonstrable familial connection between living people and the bones they claim. Mere claims for spiritual affinity with bones thousands of years old are meaningless and nothing but an anti-intellectual ploy") (Gummerman 1987: 1).

In 1990, Lynne Goldstein and Keith Kintigh, representatives of the SAA's Reburial Committee, approached the problem of reburial, stating that the issue of reburial "cannot be solved strictly as a matter of ethics" (1990: 587), and argued for a change in the way archaeologists have dealt with Native Americans—"We must change the way we do business without abrogating our responsibilities to the archaeological record or the living descendants of the people we study" (590).

But archaeologists were not the only group studying the issue of reburial and repatriation. The American Anthropological Association's Reburial Commission was an outgrowth of an ad hoc committee set up to study, report, and offer guidelines in regard to American Indian requests to rebury ancestral remains and associated grave goods held in museums, universities, and other depositories for research purposes. In its report in March 1991, it provided an overview of the development of American anthropology and offered suggestions to "guide activities at the local and national levels" (American Anthropological Association 1991a: 28). Among these were involvement of Indian people in the processes of decision making; more networking between the Indian and anthropological communities; better education about the historical usefulness of archaeology and biological anthropology; encouragement of social science training for Native Americans; development of tribal and intertribal museums and cultural centers; and the production of timely reports and films on archaeological work that is interesting to nonspecialists. In closing, they state that "the issue of human remains is not a simple issue of human rights or respect for the dead" (28).

Ultimately, the quest for understanding and the development of informal policies regarding the repatriation of human remains ended in the passage of the National Museum of the American Indian Act (NMAIA) in 1989 and the Native American Graves Protection and Repatriation Act (NAGPRA) of 1990.

It is necessary to note at this point that not all American Indian groups wish to obtain skeletal material held in museums and other collections. The Zuni Tribal Council, in Resolution No. M70-

90-LO17 (issued November 16, 1989) asked museums and other institutions to respectfully care for and curate any Zuni ancestral human remains. In the tribal view, these remains have been desecrated by their removal, and there are no adequate measures to reverse or mitigate the desecration (Society of Professional Archaeologists 1990: 3).

However, not all encounters between archaeologists and American Indians ended in protest. Roderick Sprague (1974) describes the analysis and reburial of skeletal remains encountered during construction of water and sewage lines in Weippe, Idaho, and during a cemetery relocation project in the Lower Granite Dam Reservoir. Both projects involved the Nez Perce Tribe. In the Lower Granite Dam project, the "graves were located and excavated by teams of University archaeologists and tribal members working together. The skeletal remains were analyzed by physical anthropologists and then reburied on tribal land with appropriate ceremony" (2), but this cooperation was indeed the exception rather than the rule.

REPATRIATION OF CULTURAL MATERIALS

Although American Indian groups attempted to recover items of cultural importance (i.e., the Zuni war gods from the Millicent Rogers Museum, the Denver Art Museum, and the Smithsonian Institution; and wampum belts from the State Museum of New York), most issues have dealt with those items associated with human remains (funerary objects or "grave goods"). Questions have been raised about the ownership of these objects, and about whether the objects associated with human remains should be returned with those human remains. Arguments about the scientific importance of the material, the insecure nature of many American Indian–owned museums, the insecure nature of determining ownership (individual versus tribal, tribal versus tribal, and so forth) and the legal status of museum ownership were first analyzed by Bowen Blair (1979), who ultimately stated that the best way to protect Indian artifacts is to prevent their removal from tribal lands by preventing excavation or protecting against looting (similar to King's argument in 1972).

With the passage of the NMAIA in 1989, items in the Smithsonian Institution were subjected to repatriation legislation, and a March 4, 1991, policy on the repatriation of Native American human remains and cultural materials committed "the museum to the disposition, in accordance with the wishes of *culturally based* Native Americans, of human remains . . . funerary objects; and objects transferred to or acquired . . . illegally . . . or under circumstances that render the museum's claim to them invalid" (American Anthropological Association 1991b: 1, emphasis added). Robert Adams, secretary of the Smithsonian Institution, stated "whereas anthropologists were on one side and tribal people were on the other . . . many are recognizing we can get together and work to our mutual benefit" (34).

While the policy is similar to NAGPRA, it went further in setting forth a number of principles regarding the handling and treatment of objects. Basically, the goals of the policy were to "support the continuation of ceremonial and ritual life among Native Americans, to support Native Americans who wish to study their own traditions, and to forge a consensus between the museum and Native American communities" (1991b: 1).

In October 1990, with the passage of NAGPRA, Congress established procedures that allowed American Indians to request material held in museums and federal agencies. The act, discussed in more detail in chapter 4 and only summarized here, states that, following a designated ranking of "affiliation," material culture recovered from a marked or unmarked grave shall become the property of the affiliate. It also sets forth a format to be followed when human remains are to be excavated or removed pursuant to a permit issued under Section 4 of the Archaeological Resources Protection Act of 1979 (93 Stat. 721; 16 U.S.C. 470aa et. seq.).

NAGPRA impacts not only new excavations, but also the results of previous excavations and archaeological projects. Unassociated funerary objects, sacred objects (as defined by the cultural group) or objects of cultural patrimony are subject to the same sets of regulations. Museum professionals were concerned with the passage of legislation that allowed tribal groups to regain their important artifacts, but others took a wider perspective on the issue.

In "A Philosophical Perspective on the Ethics and Resolution of Cultural Properties Issues" (quoted in Messenger 1989), Karen

Warren suggested that those involved with the study and preservation of the past should turn their views toward an integrated perspective on cultural issues to encourage all of us to "rethink the dispute as one of preservation (not, or not simply, one of ownership) of the past" (22). In this sense, the importance rests more on the preservation of an object for the sake of cultural heritage rather than on which individual (or institution) retains (or regains) the physical object in question.

SUMMARY

Archaeologists, among them Elden Johnson, confronted the conflict between American Indians and archaeologists in 1973: "These protesters say, in effect, that the responsibility acknowledged, but not always met, by the ethnographer toward the people studied is a responsibility that the professional archaeologist must also meet, and to meet it, the archaeologist must first recognize it" (Johnson 1973: 129).

Bruce Trigger argued that "the most important single factor that has shaped the long-term development of American archaeology has been the traditional Euro-American stereotype which portrayed America's native peoples as being inherently unprogressive," and that, as a result of the "relative lack of direct contact between archaeologists and native peoples, popular stereotypes have influenced archaeologists more than they have influenced ethnologists" (1980: 662). The thesis of his essay may be summarized as follows: "By eliminating the white man's definition of history as studying himself and of anthropology as the science of allegedly simpler peoples, archaeology may at last transcend some of the false consciousness that is a heritage from America's colonial past. It is our duty to recognize this heritage for what it is and overcome it" (673).

Joseph C. Winter's view of the American Indian and archaeologist controversy seems more to the point: "This confrontation is basically a conflict of values in which the representatives of competing cultures hold radically differing views of resource definition, ownership, significance, and use" (1980: 124). In 1984, he continued to discuss this conflict—"our cultural resource laws and policies regarding preservation and excavation, our other forms of

management of scientifically significant resources, and our perceptions of Indian cultures and sites as objects of study all reflect definite cultural biases" (1984: 40).

Deloria's *Custer Died for Your Sins* marks a watershed event in the
history of American anthropology. Its appearance forced anthropologists to became more aware of the feelings that American
Indians held toward them. Nearly thirty years later, under the
editorship of Thomas Biolsi and Larry Zimmerman, *Indians and
Anthropologists: Vine Deloria Jr., and the Critique of Anthropology* (1997)
presents the views of a group of anthropologists on the impact that
Deloria's writings had on them personally and on American anthropology in general. Of particular importance to archaeology,
McGuire (1997: 63–91) and Zimmerman (92–112) recall how the way
they practiced anthropology changed based on their readings of
Deloria's writings.

While these authors discuss the challenges that archaeology has
met and also those that it has failed, they recognize that the discipline has taken strides to try to ensure that American Indian concerns are aired openly. Meanwhile, national archaeology organizations continue to make strides in helping ensure that American
Indian concerns are at least acknowledged. The SAA, for example,
established a Task Force on Native American Relations at its 55th
annual meeting in Las Vegas to "advise the society on how to make
a programmatic beginning in bettering its communications and
working relationships with Native American communities"
(Watkins 1995: 14). Ultimately, the task force was reformed into the
current Committee on Native American Relations in 1995.

At the meetings of the SAA in 1996, three linked sessions ("Native Americans and Archaeology" organized by Kurt Dongoske and
Roger Anyon; "Roles and Relevancy: Native American Perspectives
on Archaeology" organized by Nina Swidler and Alan Downer; and
"Stepping Stones to Common Ground: Native Americans, Archae-
ologists, and Consultation" organized by Joe Watkins and Lynn
Larson) were devoted to exploring the relations between American
Indians and archaeologists. The fact that these sessions were pro-
posed independently of one another and later organized into a
meaningful series was an indication of the need for such discussion.
The papers of the symposia were edited and published as *Native
Americans and Archaeologists: Stepping Stones to Common Ground*
(Swidler et al. 1997).

Additionally, while the SAA's *Bulletin* had initiated a "Working Together" column in 1993 to document and chronicle the attempts of archaeologists to further involve American Indians in their work, under the editorship of Kurt Dongoske it explored not only the successes but also the pitfalls of working with tribes.

But in spite of the amount of work done by the discipline to reach a unified front, anthropologists will always have their own reasons for dealing with Native American human remains. Needless to say, there are probably as many opposed to any form of reburial as there are those in favor of controlled reburial. No one organization (e.g., the American Anthropological Association, the SAA, or the Society for Historic Archaeology) can ever hope to speak for all anthropologists or archaeologists, nor should one.

Clement Meighan, in an essay entitled "Archaeology: Science or Sacrilege?" warns that "Serious conflicts will continue, however, until a clear-cut judicial decision defines the rights and obligations of archaeological study. For the present, archaeologists can work with the existing statements of ethics and standards as published by the national archaeological organizations" (1984: 223).

Alfonso Ortiz, a Tewa Indian anthropologist, provides the caveat, "To anthropologists I say, put your own house in order because what you regard today as just a skirmish with Indians may tomorrow become a worldwide problem" (1972: 12). He concludes: "problems have to be understood before they can be solved, and I should like to think this is one of the things anthropology is all about" (12).

As has been suggested, the relationship between the American Indian and the field of historic preservation is tenuous at best. There have been successes, but, as a rule, American Indians tend to equate archaeologists with pot hunters, grave looters, or, even worse, animals who feast off of the dead (i.e., "The Vulture Culture"). Most do not trust the system supposedly designed to protect their heritage.

In the next two chapters, I examine the philosophical and legal bases that control the practice of American archaeology. For the purposes of this book, I choose to divide the practice of archaeology in two areas: anthropological archaeology (broad, academic-based archaeology, which practices archaeology primarily with a research orientation) and compliance archaeology (a business- or government-based archaeology aimed primarily at providing compliance to federal regulations with a more applied orientation). While most practitioners recognize that compliance archaeology should contain at least a minor research component, research is not its primary function.

As a result, the following discussion is perhaps naively separated into a presentation of the body of ethics that govern more the actions of the anthropological archaeologist and a presentation of the federal legislation that governs more the compliance archaeologist.

This should not be taken to imply that I feel compliance archaeologists do not adhere to a general set of ethics, or that academic archaeologists are not bound by federal regulations, but only that compliance archaeologists are more controlled by federal regulations than ethics statements in the normal practice of their business. In the eventuality of a conflict between federal law and society ethics statements, the compliance archaeologist must obey the letter of the law or risk the possibility of legal action. On the other hand, academic archaeologists come under the strictures of statutory compliance primarily if they choose to participate in compliance archaeology or choose to conduct research in geographic or academic areas where governmental regulations (e.g., federal permits, specialized curation agreements, or tribal requirements) are required.

And while neither chapter professes to present the entirety of either ethics or legislation, each one does provide a foundation for the beginning student of archaeology, ethics, compliance archaeology, or Native American relations, as well as a workable overview for the more advanced reader.

2

o~o⋈o~o

Ethics in Anthropology and Archaeology

Statements of ethics and standards for professional training are
worthwhile vehicles through which a profession can grope its way
toward a sense of fairness and responsibility. (Rosen 1980: 16)

Anthropology did not have a written set of guidelines either
delineating or suggesting its own set of moral principles or
values prior to 1948, when the Society for Applied Anthropology
(SfAA) formulated the first statement on ethics for a professional
anthropological association. However, the first conflict over
ethics in any anthropological situation came almost thirty years
previously.

In 1919, Franz Boas, founder of the American Folklore Society, the
American Ethnological Association, and the American Anthropological Association, protested the wartime activities of four anthropologists who had combined intelligence-gathering for the government with their anthropological research. Boas raised not only the
issue that the scientists had failed their science by using it as a cover
for spying activities, but also that they had thereby made it more
difficult for others engaged in "honest" work to carry on their re-
searches in foreign countries. Though Boas's charges were never
investigated, the Executive Council of the Anthropological Society
of Washington voted to censure Boas, possibly because of the
publicity and wide attention he brought to the matter. Carolyn

Fluehr-Lobban (1991: 18) raises the issue that the flaw in the action taken by the Anthropological Society of Washington was not Boas's censure so much as their quieting Boas's voice of protest and failure to debate appropriate standards of professional conduct for anthropologists.

During World War II, however, anthropology placed its members at the disposal of the government in order to bring about the successful prosecution of the war. This effort sparked studies of "national character" and studies of "culture at a distance," and produced notable works, among them Ruth R. Benedict's research into Japanese cultural that ultimately appeared as *The Chrysanthemum and the Sword* (1946). No professional protest of the governmental use of anthropologists for wartime research was forthcoming, and anthropology apparently settled into a quiet truce with governmental agencies.

During this same period, in 1941, the SfAA was established. It focused on the idea of relating anthropology to a variety of social problems, human relations, and organizational structures. Their statement on ethics in 1948 has been noted.

After World War II, anthropological employment within the government was essentially a continuation of the war effort, with research in Micronesia, Africa, and other "less developed" areas of the globe. This period of time, after World War II and into the Vietnam War era, was one of growing public acceptance of the field of anthropology.

Project Camelot, a government-sponsored project designed to address the problem of counterinsurgency in Latin America, also attempted to understand the ways that knowledge gained through the social sciences could be used to assist the army in coping with internal revolutions in the region (Fluehr-Lobban 1991: 23). The reaction of anthropologists to this project and the resulting furor over even innocent government-sponsored research led to the 1967 Statement on Problems of Anthropological Research and Ethics, which centered on the issue of clandestine research and government contracts.

In 1968, the Executive Board of the American Anthropological Association (AAA) appointed an official Interim Committee on Ethics to develop the standing committee on ethics and to make recommendations regarding the nature of relationships anthropologists should have with one another and with other bodies they might impact. Subsequently, a nine-member standing Committee on Ethics was elected in 1970.

In March 1970, Eric Wolf, chair of the AAA's Committee on Ethics, and Joseph Jorgensen, a member of the committee, received information about the wartime activities of anthropologists in Thailand. The information was published before the AAA could handle it internally, but the AAA reaction was similar to the 1919 action— it publicly censured Wolf and Jorgensen more severely than those whose professional behavior was called into question. Later that year, the standing Committee on Ethics published its revised draft code, Statement of Professional Responsibility, which was subsequently adopted by the membership as the Principles of Professional Responsibility in 1971.

The code spoke to six responsibilities of the individual anthropologist: (a) to those studied, (b) to the discipline, (c) to the public, (d) to students, (e) to sponsors, and (f) to one's own and host governments.

The first of these responsibilities, relations with those studied, is of direct relevance to this study. It states that anthropologists' *paramount* responsibility is to those they study—not to their sponsoring institution, host government, or even to their science. It also affirms that when there is a conflict, the individual must come first.

After the decline in employment opportunities in academia in the mid-1970s, the AAA Committee on Ethics was asked to revise the code to meet the needs of a profession that was no longer centered in university research. This resulted in the proposal and publication in October 1984 of a new code of ethics, entitled the Draft Code of Ethics, which openly stated it would not address the many ethical responsibilities anthropologists face either as academics or workers with outside sponsors, but was proposed primarily to establish a framework within which disclosures of ethical problems and debate on ethical issues could be conducted within the established framework of anthropology. The draft revision was not accepted by the membership.

Another revision of the principles was proposed in 1989 and accepted in 1990. The new General Principles of Professional Responsibility did not amount to a major revision of the previous principles, but it did remove all references to clandestine and secret research.

Up to this time, most of the AAA's dealings with ethics had been influenced by stress during or relating to times of war—rarely was anything done without the impetus provided by such national activity. The failure of the discipline to act after the initial Boas conflict appears to have set the pace for the development of the body of ethics in the discipline.

It is also obvious that the lack of an organized body of ethics relating to American Indians or other native groups (such as the Micronesian societies) was influenced by the concern not about who was studied, nor how the study was carried out, but rather the funding source or motivation behind the study.

However, the question of ethics in anthropology became worthy of study itself, as noted by a series of articles published under the "Lessons for the Field—Ethics in Fieldwork" column in the AAA's *Anthropology Newsletter* in 1993–1994, followed by a series of more general essays and articles in the column entitled "Ethical Dilemmas." This column was replaced by "Ethical Currents" in September 1998.

With the unanimous approval by the AAA Executive Board in May 1995 that "[t]he AAA no longer adjudicate claims of unethical behavior and focus its efforts and resources on an ethics education program" (Commission to Review the AAA Statements on Ethics, Final Report), the purpose of the AAA Code of Ethics shifted to education of the practitioner prior to the development of a problem.

From January 1995 through March 1997, the Commission to Review the AAA's Statement on Ethics worked on producing new professional guidelines for AAA members. Open hearings were held at the 1995 and 1996 annual meetings of the AAA, and the commission additionally solicited comments from all AAA sections (with drafts discussed at the 1995 and 1996 section assemblies).

The final report of the commission was published in the *Anthropology Newsletter* (September 1995), with drafts of the new code published in the April 1996 and annual meeting editions of the *Newsletter*. The membership voted on the New AAA Code of Ethics in the spring 1998 ballot and approved it in June 1998.

The shift in intent of the code regarding the people anthropologists study is notable. In the Principles of Professional Responsibility, anthropologists are warned that their paramount responsibility was to those they study (principle 1), while, in the current AAA code, practitioners are advised that they have "ethical obligations to the people, species, and material they study and to the people with whom they work" (III[A][1]).

In dealing with human subjects, the code focuses on "Conservation, Consultation, and Consent." It exhorts the anthropologist to "work for the long-term conservation of the archaeological, fossil, and historical records"; to "consult actively with the affected individuals or group(s), with the goal of establishing a working relationship that can be beneficial to all parties involved"; and to seek "informed consent" from the persons being studied in advance of fieldwork.

Therefore, the AAA's Code of Ethics has evolved from a more restrictive document that set out to govern the professional conduct of anthropologists into a document that attempts only to provide guidelines for individual anthropologist's actions.

ARCHAEOLOGY

As a subdiscipline of anthropology, archaeology has struggled with defining the ethical structure to be imposed on its practitioners since the establishment of the Society for American Archaeology (SAA) in 1934. Beginning with its initial constitution and by-laws, the SAA was established to prevent the "practice of securing, hoarding, exchanging, buying, or selling of archaeological objects . . ." for personal satisfaction or profit (Article I, Section 2). Article III, Section 10, gives the society the right to drop from the rolls of the society anyone who habitually commercializes archaeological objects or sites (Society for American Archaeology 1977: 308–12).

Additional guidance to archaeologists was provided in 1961. "Four Statements for Archaeology" set guidelines for accepted standards in delineating the field of archaeology, the methods of archaeology, ethics for archaeology, and recommendations for training in archaeology (Champe et al. 1961: 137–38). These statements provided SAA members with an idea of what may be considered right and wrong, at least in the eyes of the SAA, and provided guidelines to the SAA Executive Committee relating to the expulsion of a member.

The Society of Professional Archaeologists (SOPA) developed out of an ad hoc committee on standards appointed by the SAA to pursue the concept of certifying archaeologists (McGimsey and Davis 1977: 97–105). This society allowed only those archaeologists meeting certain criteria to be admitted, required applicants to sign a Code of Ethics and Standards of Research Performance, and provided a detailed procedure for review of alleged violations.

Discussions of ethical issues continued in spite of the fact that only one society (SOPA) had a formalized code of ethics.

In 1984, Ernestine L. Green edited a collection of essays dealing with the differing ways archaeologists view their work and why they continue to pursue archaeology as a career. Her *Ethics and Values in Archaeology* presented essays in a collective approach to a rarely discussed topic.

Hester A. Davis's essay, "Approaches to Ethical Problems by Archaeological Organizations" (1984), was primarily a historical overview of formal codes of ethics in archaeology, their intended function, and the extent to which they had worked.

Later, in 1988, Calvin R. Cummings compared and discussed the ethical codes or statements of behavior (either as separate standards or within their by-laws) of seven major professional archaeological societies in the United States: the SAA, the Society for Historical Archaeology (SHA), the American Society for Conservation Archaeology (ASCA), the National Association of State Archaeologists (NASA), the SOPA—now known as the Register of Professional Archaeologists (RPA)—the Association of Field Archaeologists (AFA), and the Archaeological Institute of America (AIA).

These statements "collectively form the discipline's framework and focal point for archaeology in the United States" (Cummings 1988: 1) and deal with the aims of archaeology to prevent the commercialization of archaeological sites, the treatment of artifacts, and the presentation of data. Only in the RPA Codes of Ethics (1.1[c]) are archaeologists specifically told to be "sensitive to, and respect the legitimate concerns of, groups whose culture histories are the subjects of archaeological investigations."

But the changing milieu in which archaeology is practiced led the SAA to reexamine its stance on ethics and the practice of archaeology in 1993. At a two-day workshop in Reno, members of the SAA's Committee on Ethics and a number of advisors to the committee developed a series of six principles that were designed to begin a broad process of consultation with the practitioners of the discipline in order to develop a more workable set of ethics (Lynott and Wylie 1995).

These principles—stewardship, accountability, commercialization, public education and outreach, intellectual property, and records and preservation—were presented in a symposium at the Anaheim meetings of the SAA in 1994, at various regional archaeological meetings throughout the United States, and discussed in detail in a special publication of the SAA edited by Mark Lynott and Alison Wylie, entitled *Ethics in American Archaeology: Challenges for the 1990s* (1995).

However, it is important to note that not all of the authors in the book were directly supportive of the principles. Christopher Hamilton (1995: 57–63) discussed a different interpretation of "commercialism" and questioned the prohibition of working with salvors to rescue the information from salvaged shipwrecks; Larry Zimmerman (64–67) noted that archaeologists, as self-appointed stewards of the past, perhaps are deluding themselves into thinking that only archaeologists have the ability to protect the past; and Janet Levy (1995: 86–93) discussed the SAA's principles and their relation to the AAA's Principles of Professional Responsibility.

As a result of the consultation started with the publication and presentation of the principles, two additional principles, Public Reporting and Publication and Training and Resources, were developed. Lynott (1997) gives a short history and overall development of the SAA's Ethics Policy.

Of the codes examined by Cummings in 1988 and the new Principles of Archaeological Ethics, the RPA's code is the most restrictive to archaeologists. But the question remains: Should *every* archaeologist be subjected to a code of ethics as strict as the RPA code?

An examination of the Code of Scientific Ethics of the Society for California Archaeology is much stronger regarding communication with Native Americans. Section 4 discusses the shared commitment to the preservation of archaeological remains, and encourages members of the society to contact representatives of the community during the planning phases of projects in order to develop a fieldwork design that will have the least impact on the interests and sensitivities of the Native Americans (part A); proscribes society members from excavating or disturbing current or recent Native American locales (communities, cemeteries, and so forth) without full agreement by the Native Americans involved (part B); and the reinterment (after analysis) of skeletal remains known to have been interred after A.D. 1800, in compliance with relevant state and local statutes (part C).

Such a nationwide policy would scarcely impact the conduct of archaeological research other than to increase the amount of lead time necessary prior to actual field research. The codification of an informal policy of communication and consultation may be necessary if the discipline is to step beyond its current bounds in the quest for strong ethics in relation to native peoples of the United States.

While these sets of ethical codes have been established by major groups within the United States, one worldwide group has also established codes of conduct to which it feels ethical archaeologists should adhere. The first meeting of the World Archaeological Congress in Southampton, England, in 1986, addressed archaeology in its widest sense, and called together not only academics from various countries but also nonacademics from a wide range of cultural backgrounds (Ucko 1994: ix).

In August 1989, a meeting was held to discuss the topics of reburial and repatriation. At the Inter-Congress on Archaeological Ethics and the Treatment of the Dead in Vermillion, South Dakota, presentations focused on aspects of the issue ranging from the approaches taken by biological anthropologists to the feelings that indigenous populations have about the spirits of the dead. On the final day, the so-called Vermillion Accord was passed.

The accord contained six clauses:

1. Respect for the mortal remains of the dead shall be accorded to all irrespective of origin, race, religion, nationality, custom, and tradition.
2. Respect for the wishes of the dead concerning disposition shall be accorded whenever possible, reasonable, and lawful, when they are known or can be reasonably inferred.
3. Respect for the wishes of the local community and of relatives or guardians of the dead shall be accorded whenever possible, reasonable, and lawful.
4. Respect for the scientific research value of skeletal, mummified, and other human remains (including fossil hominids) shall be accorded when such value is demonstrated to exist.
5. Agreement to the disposition of fossil, skeletal, mummified, and other remains shall be reached by negotiation on the ba-

sis of mutual respect for the legitimate concerns of communities for the proper disposition of their ancestors as well as the legitimate concerns of science and education.
6. Express recognition that the concerns of various ethnic groups, as well as those of science, are legitimate and to be respected, will permit acceptable agreements to be reached and honored. (Zimmerman and Bruguier 1994: 6)

At the World Archaeological Congress II in Barquisimeto, Venezuela, in 1990, members adopted a First Code of Ethics: Members' Obligations to Indigenous Peoples, with eight Principles to Abide By and seven Rules to Adhere To (for a complete text, see Zimmerman and Bruguier [1994: 6–7]). "The fundamental notion behind the code," say the authors, "is that it gives direction to archaeology in the profession's dealings with indigenous peoples" (1994: 8).

The previous discussion has been a very brief summation relating the history of the development of the body of ethics of the anthropological and archaeological communities. Even though the first ethical conflicts did not relate to the study of American Indian groups or the remains of those groups (identified or unidentified), they have become the common subjects of ethical dilemmas. Of nearly equal importance is the material result of the excavations.

CULTURAL PROPERTY

Probably the first organized attempt at regaining cultural property by an American Indian group began in 1969 with the Onondaga attempt to regain their wampum belts. The conflict was reported in newspapers (*Watertown Daily Times, Akwesasne Notes*), as well as in scholarly journals (*Anthropology Newsletter, The Indian Historian*). Anthropologists were on both sides of the conflict, with Jack A. Frisch, Robert A. Thomas, and Anthony F. C. Wallace supporting the idea of return of cultural artifacts and the Council on Anthropological Research in Museums decrying their return.

The Onondaga eventually did receive the belts when the New York State Assembly voted their return and after an Indian-owned and controlled museum had been established for the protection and curation of the artifacts. But the battle over the control of the artifacts shook many professionals whose livelihood depended upon the American Indian, from anthropologists and archaeologists to those in the museum professions.

The fight over the wampum belts was one of the first salvos from American Indian groups for the control of their own history and their cultural artifacts. American Indians were no longer content to allow the anthropological or museum communities to determine what was to be displayed, how the material was to be interpreted, and the limits of Indian involvement in the entire preservation process.

In 1971, James D. Nason, then curator of ethnology at the Thomas Burke Memorial Washington State Museum at the University of Washington, discussed the relationship between museums and American Indians. He outlined three basic criticisms that he had heard American Indian groups make against museums:

> The materials, some or all, were collected in the past by either immoral or illicit means. We have amassed such collections to satisfy societal drives based on materialistic greed or, perhaps worse, cultural imperialism. And, we seek to maintain collections in such a way that Indians are excluded from any contact with or relationship with their material heritage. (1971: 14)

He goes on to suggest the return of cultural specimens to indigenous peoples after certain conditions have been met, among them that the items are culturally significant, that an adequate facility is available for their storage and protection, that trained personnel and stabilized funding is available, and that the materials would revert to museum stewardship should any of the previously mentioned conditions no longer be met (1971: 17).

Another museum professional, Delbert J. McBride, curator of the State Capitol Museum in Olympia, Washington, discussed the ways that museums could better increase their relations with American Indian groups. In an essay entitled "The Ethics of Ethnic Collections," he wrote: "There are many positive ways in which museums can become involved with living Indians, rather than by confining all our efforts to artifacts of the nineteenth century" (1971: 11).

Both of these museum professionals were interested in the relationships between American Indian groups and the "business" of museums, and both provided discussions about dealing with the desires of native groups for the return of materials in museum collections.

T. J. Ferguson's essay "Archaeological Ethics and Values in a Tribal Cultural Resource Management Program at the Pueblo of Zuni" (1984) provides a different viewpoint relative to artifacts held in museum collections. After giving a brief history of the archaeological program at Zuni, Ferguson writes: "One of the key ethical issues involved with the management of sacred cultural resources is making sure that the people responsible for the religious artifacts or sites participate in the decisions made about them" (233–34).

The Zuni believe that when there exists a conflict between the religious use of an artifact and its scientific or artistic use, the religious value supersedes all others. It is also understood that, among the Zuni, some things must remain secret in order to retain their sacredness.

E. Charles Adams, writing about his involvement with the Hopi during the Walpi project, also expounds upon the American Indian's right to control the material that comes from reservation lands:

> When archaeologists work with Native Americans, they should be willing to communicate and compromise. Strict adherence to professional standards that make no sense to the Native American, or, in fact, violate the beliefs of his culture may jeopardize the specific project, as well as future projects in the area, and damage the image of the archaeologist. . . . There is seldom a need to compromise archaeological values. (1984: 241–42)

Phyllis Mauch Messenger's book, *The Ethics of Collecting Cultural Property: Whose Culture? Whose Property?* (1989), approaches the question of ownership, "cultural patrimony," and other issues. The chapter cowritten by Deborah L. Nichols, Anthony L. Klesert, and Roger Anyon, entitled "Ancestral Sites, Shrines, and Graves: Native American Perspectives on the Ethics of Collecting Cultural Properties," supposedly approaches the question (1989: 27–38). However, it is mostly an essay about "looting" and "pot hunting" on the various reservations where the authors work, and does not address the subject of "scientific collection." The authors conclude that "the Native American ethic—one that respects the power and authority of these remains and eschews the possibility of 'ownership' by anyone—is the only defensible position to take towards the heritage of the past" (37).

Among most professional archaeologists in North America, commerce in artifacts and antiquities is considered to be unethical. This works to conserve the critical resource in that scientists try to prevent the marketing of artifacts and the related destruction of those archaeological sites from which they are excavated. Archaeologists work to acquire and preserve archaeological information, most of which is derived from artifacts and their context. Archaeologists, in general, are not in the business for the artifacts alone, but they depend upon those artifacts to provide information about the society that produced them. Most professional archaeological societies (see Cummings 1988) caution against the use and abuse of artifacts for personal or financial gain, but is it any wonder that native peoples and nonprofessionals place importance on the *product* of a culture instead of the culture, when archaeologists may unknowingly mislead them in displays and educational programs by placing emphasis on the artifact instead of the information it provides? Programs aimed at relating the information artifacts tell are worthwhile, but rarely are they filled with the "common" materials obtained from excavations (such as the byproducts of lithic tool production).

Most issues regarding the repatriation of artifacts seem balanced around the issue of "Who really owns the artifact?" This question is not only being raised in the United States, but also in industrialized countries throughout the world. The situation regarding the status of indigenous populations and repatriation of human remains and artifacts in other portions of the world is discussed in chapter 10, but a brief example is presented here.

Christopher Anderson notes that the request for repatriation of artifacts by local, indigenous populations does not always result in the wholesale decimation of collections (1990: 54–55). In dealing with the Aboriginals of southern Australia, he found that, following the development of social networks between the Aboriginals and museum professionals, the Aboriginals actually loaned more objects to the South Australian Museum in Adelaide for protection, storage, and/or safekeeping, and provided information on other artifacts, rather than removing artifacts from collections as the museum community had initially feared.

SUMMARY

Although no set of ethics can be established that can provide answers for *every* set of circumstances, archaeology has only superficially provided guidance to individual archaeologists about their relationships with native peoples. Most of the energy expended in the direction of ethics relates to the "proper" conduct of science, the "proper" methods of gathering data, the "proper" ways to curate the data, and the "proper" way to deal with colleagues, students, clients, and employer/employees.

But it is encouraging that numerous archaeologists and anthropologists offer classes on the ethical practice of anthropology. These classes expose graduate and undergraduate anthropology students to the complex sets of issues with which anthropologists must grapple and examine the various means by which the discipline has attempted to define the ethical anthropologist.

Indiana University at Bloomington went beyond merely offering classes to students by developing a programmatic approach at providing training in these issues. A new program, initiated in the fall of 1998 and explained in the Indiana University Department of Anthropology *1999 Graduate Student Guide*, offers a Ph.D. track in archaeology in the social context. This program bridges the subfields of social/cultural anthropology and archaeology to address archaeological issues as they apply to contemporary people. The course of study provides students with a general background in anthropology coupled with a broad knowledge of the fields of social/cultural anthropology and archaeology, including theoretical issues and field/laboratory methods. Students are expected to develop individualized interest areas that include, but are not limited to, cultural property, public archaeology, archaeological ethics, heritage management, and repatriation.

Course requirements include archaeological ethics, issues in archaeology and social context, "methods" courses, and courses in culture areas. A practicum or internship is also suggested.

The Indiana example is strongly oriented toward providing training in issues that face current archaeologists, but it is unique. Training and the formulation of strong codes governing the ethical practice of archaeology are necessary, because if archaeology (as a discipline) and individual archaeologists delay action, the informal ethical codes that exist may be formalized by legislative fiat.

The following chapter analyzes selected legislation that legislates processes that at one time were voluntary upon practitioners of compliance archaeology. In this regard, these laws and statutes have removed certain choices and require certain actions, and form a body of "legislated ethics."

3

ᴏ～ᴏ ⋈ ᴏ～ᴏ

Laws Protecting American Indian Cultural Resources

In order to understand the extent to which compliance archaeologists might have allowed their ethics to be legislated for them, it is necessary to understand the legislative background relating to cultural resource protection within the United States. Thomas F. King's two recent books on cultural resource laws and procedures (1998) and the Section 106 process of the National Historic Preservation Act (2000) offer one of the best and most readable discussions on cultural resource laws and regulations. As such, the laws will not be presented in their entirety here and the reader is referred to these two books.

However, certain points must be made. Compliance archaeology deals only with projects that utilize federal or tribal funds, are on federal or tribal lands, or require federal or tribal permits in order for the project to be undertaken. They do not (except in rare instances) apply to projects that occur on private land using private funds and that do not require a federal or tribal permit. While some states do require state permits prior to excavations, those are more the exception than the rule. Mostly, the protection of the cultural environment has been seen to be a federal rather than state responsibility.

THE LEGISLATIVE BASE

The first legislative attempt to protect cultural resources began with the passage of the Antiquities Act of 1906 (Public Law 59-209). This act provided for the protection of historic and prehistoric remains on public lands, established criminal sanctions for unauthorized destruction or appropriation of antiquities owned or controlled by the federal government, and authorized a permit system for the scientific investigation of antiquities on federal land. Although it did not mention American Indian groups specifically, it established the principle that cultural resources, regardless of origin, were important to the cultural history of the United States and deserved protection.

With the passage of the Antiquities Act, the American Indian's unwritten history and material culture began to be co-opted by the United States. While it was deemed important to protect the evidence of the cultures that had gone before, the fact that the existing tribal groups did not rate a mention in the law perhaps illustrates the amount of consideration that archaeology was giving to living groups.

The Historic Sites Act of 1935 (Public Law 74-292) designated the secretary of the interior as being responsible for establishing the National Survey of Historic Sites and Buildings, required the preservation of properties of national or archaeological significance, allowed for the designation of national historic landmarks, and authorized interagency, intergovernmental, and interdisciplinary efforts for the preservation of such resources. This act established the relationship between cultural resource preservation and the U.S. government and reaffirmed the idea that cultural resources, regardless of whose ancestors produced them, were important to the nation as a whole.

The Reservoir Salvage Act of 1960 (Public Law 86-523) provided for the recovery and preservation of historical and archaeological data that might be lost or destroyed as a result of the construction of federally funded or licensed dams, reservoirs, and attendant facilities and activities. This act established the principle that the federal government should take responsibility for actions that might impact cultural resources, and was extensively amended by the

Archaeological and Historic Preservation Act of 1974 (Public Law 93-291).

The National Historic Preservation Act of 1966 (Public Law 89-665) set forth a national policy of historic preservation, directed the expansion of the National Register of Historic Places to include resources of regional, state, and local as well as national significance, established the president's Advisory Council on Historic Preservation, and encouraged the states to conduct statewide surveys and to prepare "state historic preservation plans." It also authorized the secretary of the interior to provide grants to support surveys, planning, and preservation activities. Finally, it set up procedures (Section 106) that must be followed by federal agencies in the event that a proposed project might affect significant properties. Public Law 94-422 amended the act in 1976.

The law itself is regulated through 36 CFR 60 and 36 CFR 800, Procedures for the Protection of Historic and Cultural Properties. 36 CFR 60 defines appropriate terms and detailed the procedures involved in nominating sites to the National Register. It also requires states to provide at least one public notice as well as a reasonable time for comment prior to placing a site on the National Register. 36 CFR 800 sets forth both the review procedures for the determination of affect and the power of the president's Advisory Council to comment upon all such instances. Both regulations list the criteria for determining whether a property is eligible for the National Register.

Prior to 1980, the act had no specific references to Indian tribes. Public Law 96-515 amended the act, giving Indian tribes equal ranking with state and local governments as a partner, authorized grants to Indian tribes for the preservation of their cultural heritage, and added Section 110, which set forth minimum responsibilities for federal agencies. In 1992, the Fowler Bill (Public Law 102-575) amendments allowed properties of traditional religious or cultural importance to native groups to be included in the National Register determination process, and provided for the establishment of tribal preservation offices. More recently, in 1999, the president's Advisory Council revamped its 36 CFR Part 800 regulations dealing with implementation of Section 106 of the National Historic Preservation Act to better define the roles of the various participants in the process and to strengthen the role of American Indian groups.

The Department of Transportation Act of 1966 (Public Law 89-670, in conjunction with the Federal-Aid Highways Act of 1966, Public Law 89-574) directed the Department of Transportation to spend funds for the purposes of protecting, avoiding, or studying archaeological sites to be affected by federally supported road construction. The precedent for highway salvage archaeology, as Jessie L. Nusbaum has noted (quoted in Wendorf, Fox, and Lewis 1956: VII), began with the establishment of an archaeological program for the New Mexico Bureau of Public Roads in 1954 as an outgrowth of a similar program of salvage archaeology conducted on the Navajo Reservation for the El Paso Natural Gas San Juan Pipeline Project.

The National Environmental Policy Act of 1969 (Public Law 91-190) required evaluation of the effects of major federal actions on environmental (including cultural) resources. This act lengthened the comment and consultation period prior to the beginning of a federal undertaking by including cultural resource management in the planning rather than in the construction phase of a federal project.

Executive Order 11593 of May 13, 1971 (Protection and Enhancement of the Cultural Environment), directed all agencies to inventory historic properties under their ownership or control, to nominate eligible properties to the National Register, and to give priority in inventory to federally owned properties to be transferred or altered. It also directed federal agencies to develop policies to contribute to the preservation of all historic properties not owned or controlled by the federal government, and to exercise caution until inventories were completed to ensure that eligible properties were not inadvertently damaged or destroyed.

The Archaeological and Historic Preservation Act of 1974 (Public Law 93-291, amendment to the Reservoir Salvage Act of 1960) specifically provides a mechanism for the preservation of archaeological and historical data, outlines the actions to be taken by federal agencies undertaking or authorizing construction activities that may affect archaeological or historical properties, and authorizes the agency to transfer or expend up to 1 percent of project funds for protection of any archaeological or historical properties. The secretary of the interior was also authorized to survey and investigate areas to be impacted by construction if the undertaking agency could not provide adequate protection or investigation, as well as to receive the transfer of up to 1 percent of project budgets for the preservation of significant archaeological or historical data.

More recent legislation has changed the orientation of cultural resources managers, from object-oriented studies more to culture-oriented ones. The American Indian Religious Freedom Act of 1978 (Public Law 9zzzz5-341), the Archaeological Resources Protection Act of 1979 (Public Law 96-95), and the Native American Graves Protection and Repatriation Act of 1990 (Public Law 101-601) have legislated certain aspects of archaeology that were once personal choices.

The American Indian Religious Freedom Act of 1978 (AIRFA) required federal agencies to examine the areas where their policies and regulations affected the religious freedoms of American Indians. Although the law itself had no legislative "teeth" to it (no legislative remedies to any federal laws or guidelines that affected Indian religious practices were proposed), the relationship between archaeologists and American Indians changed as a result. A proposal to put legislative "teeth" in AIRFA was introduced into the 102nd Congress as "The American Indian Religious Freedom Resolution of 1991" but failed to reach the floor.

The Archaeological Resources Protection Act of 1979 (ARPA) was established because vague definitions in the original Antiquities Act of 1906 ultimately weakened its ability to protect the cultural resources from unauthorized excavation, removal, damage, or destruction. ARPA established provisions regarding the issuance of permits to conduct archaeological investigations on public or Indian lands. American Indians were exempted from permitting procedures under this act only if the tribe had its own cultural resources laws and if the material was on Indian land. The act also required consultation with the affected Indian tribe by anyone wishing to undertake investigations prior to the issuance of a permit, and allowed the tribe to attach its own terms and conditions to the permit.

Essentially, this act was the first to give congressional recognition to the rights of Indian tribes to regulate the excavation or removal of archaeological resources on Indian land, even though it listed skeletal remains as "cultural resources," a sore point among many American Indian groups.

The uniform regulations set up to carry out ARPA required that archaeologists develop consultation with federal land managers,

Indian tribes, representatives of state agencies, and the general public. Consideration of the provisions of AIRFA was also required. The primary purpose of the rules and regulations was to establish procedures to govern the issuance of permits.

Additionally, the final rules and regulations also required federal land managers to:

> identify all Indian tribes having aboriginal or historic ties to the lands under the Federal land manager's jurisdiction, and seek to determine, from the chief executive officer or other designated official of any such tribe, the location and nature of specific sites of religious or cultural importance so that such information may be on file for land management purposes. (16 U.S.C. 470w-3, section 69.7[b][1])

Conflicts between American Indian religious values and federal land-use practices could most likely be lessened should both groups develop an attitude of trust and understanding. Archaeologists and Indians would benefit from such an arrangement; archaeologists would be able to better protect sites from impact by projects, and American Indian groups would be ensured continued protection from accidental impacts. American Indian groups, however, are reluctant to provide information about cultural and sacred sites to most non-Indians out of a tacit fear that such information could be used to locate, impact, and possibly destroy the sites.

Ultimately, ARPA and its rules and regulations forced archaeologists and other individuals wishing to excavate, survey, or conduct archaeological research on federal or tribal lands to establish direct lines of communication with the affected tribes and to be subjected to tribal terms or conditions. It has also allowed the tribes to set up their own rules and regulations to circumvent the federal bureaucracy, as the Navajo and Zuni have done in establishing the tribal cultural resources programs and permitting procedures.

The newest piece of legislation affecting archaeology, the Native American Graves Protection and Repatriation Act of 1990 (NAGPRA) has been mentioned before and will be discussed in more detail in the next chapter. It addresses the repatriation of American Indian, Native Alaskan, and Native Hawaiian human remains, funerary objects, sacred objects, and items of cultural patrimony currently held by federal agencies and institutions that receive federal funds and defines "ownership" of human remains and items of cultural importance when excavated or otherwise found on lands under federal or tribal control by setting up a ranking of control of remains of cultural importance from individual family, related kin, and tribal group.

The law called for the inventory of all affected material within five years of the passage of the act, and required federal agencies or other institutions to consult with tribal governments and traditional religious leaders once the inventory had been completed. A review committee was set up to monitor the progress of the inventory and repatriation process. The law also established penalties if museums failed to comply with the act, and grants to Indian tribes and Native Hawaiian organizations to assist with repatriation requests and to museums to be used in the compiling of the inventories.

LEGISLATED ETHICS

The laws and regulations previously summarized form the foundation of compliance archaeology within the United States. With the Antiquities Act of 1906, it became the policy of the U.S. government to protect the cultural resources within its borders—an attempt to develop a cultural patrimony—regardless of cultural origin or wishes of the cultural groups who produced the objects involved. It was not until 1979 that American Indian tribes were given status equal to state and local governments relative to the control of those cultural resources.

These laws and regulations spell out the duties of the compliance archaeologist in a rather straightforward way: The archaeologist is to be concerned with the protection of the cultural environment and to include concerns relative to it in the planning, construction, and finalization stages of any project. Tribal groups are to be contacted, as are any federal or state agencies, that have any sort of involvement in the land upon (or within) which the cultural material is located. Additionally, the analysis of certain types of artifacts (human remains, funerary objects, sacred items, or items of cultural patrimony) may be curtailed or prevented. And, ultimately, the artifacts may be returned to the cultural groups with which the artifacts are associated.

It is impossible to weigh the impact of the last three pieces of legislation on the discipline of archaeology without the time-depth necessary to provide a track record. It is uncertain whether anthropology as a whole will alter its ways of dealing with American Indian groups, or whether archaeology, ethnology, physical anthropology, or biological anthropology will each be forced to adopt distinct procedures and guidelines in conducting research.

Chapter 1 provided a brief discussion of the basic points of conflict between American Indian groups and anthropology—the excavation of burials, both recent and ancient; the reburial of human remains and associated grave goods, and the repatriation of cultural material of a religious or sacred nature. Now we will look at how the resolution of these points of conflict has been approached through legislation, and the ways that choices open to individual archaeologists have been influenced by law.

THE EXCAVATION OF BURIALS, BOTH RECENT AND ANCIENT

The excavation of the burials of individuals of American Indian descent has been a primary point of concern between both American Indians and archaeologists, as noted by Lawrence Rosen (1980), Jane Buikstra (1981), Valerie Talmage (1982), Duane Anderson (1985), and others. Available published American Indian opinions tend to view this as a conflict between Indian and non-Indian spiritual or religious values (Deloria 1969; Quick 1985), while most archaeologists (Meighan 1984; Buikstra 1981; Talmage 1982) tend to view the problem as a conflict between scientific and nonscientific values.

As is readily apparent from chapter 1, American Indian concerns have also focused on the inconsistent application of various federal and state laws regarding the protection of human remains. In the past, unmarked American Indian graves have not been afforded the same protection that is given to unmarked non-Indian graves. The excavation of American Indian remains, considered to be an "archaeological resource" (a term repugnant to most Indian groups), will be controlled by all three new laws. Both ARPA and NAGPRA require consultation with tribal groups that can demonstrate cultural affinity, while AIRFA has had at least some influence on federal policies relative to permits for excavation and the protection afforded burials and associated grave goods.

Prior to 1980, consultation with tribes about research being carried out on tribal lands was unnecessary. Individual archaeologists usually contacted local authorities, but such contact was not required. However, such communication prior to beginning field investigations has become more and more necessary. Currently, an individual cannot conduct any cultural resource investigations on federal or tribal lands without an Antiquities' Permit, and that individual cannot get a permit without consultation with all affected parties, including American Indian groups.

Another point of concern of American Indian groups has been with the reports completed as a result of the research. American Indians have stated that they often feel that material obtained from research carried out on reservations and other Indian lands is rarely made available to the local population—that generally the material appears in some scientific publication and in scientific jargon. This complaint is often valid, and is symptomatic of the field as a whole. However, with more Indian control in permitting, surveying, and cultural resource management on federal and tribal lands, such practices will probably lessen; either that, or individual archaeologists who do not produce usable "popular reports" may be denied permits for additional work in the area.

No longer are American Indians being viewed as laboratory or museum specimens to be manipulated for scientific study. Many American Indian tribes are controlling the cultural materials within their tribal lands, and the 1980 amendments to the National Historic Preservation Act gave legislative standing to tribal groups that wished to apply for grants to conduct their own survey and inventory of cultural properties eligible for inclusion in the National Register of Historic Places. This was the initial step toward cultural resource autonomy. ARPA gave congressional recognition to the right of Indian tribes to regulate the excavation or removal of archaeological resources from tribal lands, and also required the consideration of provisions of AIRFA. Finally, NAGPRA gives tribal ownership to archaeological resources from federal or tribal lands to those tribes proving cultural affiliation as well as those materials excavated from any lands that eventually come under control of a federal agency.

If all three of the most recent laws are taken in conjunction with the National Historic Preservation Act (with amendments), it is possible that American Indians can control *all* excavations on federal lands, as well as a major portion of any human remains recovered to date or in the future. The development of the NAGPRA inventories of cultural materials held in museums that receive federal funds may be a temporary boon to researchers in material culture as well as to archaeologists, since at least some analysis and study of materials scheduled for repatriation is necessary.

Again, voluntary ethical choices are lessened. Decisions relative to the archaeological study of an Indian group now must be made with the group rather than apart from the group. There will still be the opportunity to study cultural material found on private lands without facing the consultation requirements, but these situations may become less and less common.

The focus of this chapter so far has been on federal laws that deal with cultural resources and their management. However, in some instances, state and local laws may be more restrictive. In North Dakota, for example, it is a Class B felony to disturb a burial as well as a misdemeanor if an individual knows of a burial location but does not report it (Del Bene and Banks 1990).

North Dakota House Bill 1584 established an Intertribal Reinterment Committee to deal with American Indian human remains. Among some of the requirements set up by the law, the investigators must be qualified archaeologists, and analyses must be done *in situ*, with no excavation, radiometric measurements, DNA analyses, or other intrusive procedures allowed. When burials discovered as a result of a project have already been disturbed, photographs and other visual procedures (no intrusive tests) are allowed. No photographs of any American Indian burial may be published. Also, the committee allows up to sixty days for the study of a single burial, and up to ninety days for the study of multiple burials. If an individual burial can be identified by name, the remains come under the control of the Health Services rather than an archaeologist, with reinterment on Indian lands.

THE REBURIAL OF HUMAN REMAINS AND ASSOCIATED GRAVE GOODS; AND THE REPATRIATION OF CULTURAL MATERIAL OF A RELIGIOUS OR SACRED NATURE

The final two points will be discussed together since they are closely related, deeply personal, and essentially form almost a single point of concern.

American Indian religious views about the handling and treatment of human remains and associated materials vary widely, as do the views of non-Indian religions. To speak of a "universal Indian view of religion" is as impossible as trying to condense all world religions into a single statement. However, it seems that American Indians no longer need to be able to justify their positions relative to the reburial of human remains, the repatriation of associated grave goods, or the repatriation of sacred or religious items—currently, the only requirement necessary is evidence of cultural affinity.

Even prior to the passage of NAGPRA, the idea of repatriation led many archaeologists to believe that all excavations would be controlled by radical Indians claiming religious infringement (Meighan 1984), that physical anthropologists decried the potential loss of a large and necessary (in their view) database (Buikstra 1981), and that ethnologists and museologists were afraid of losing a large body of cultural material from museum collections. In short, the scientific community, beginning with the discussion of the repatriation of the Onondaga wampum belts in 1970, rose against the perceived threat to their databases—material culture and human remains alike—from those whose ancestors had produced the databases.

Scientists have been forced to reexamine their own ethical positions by defining the extent that they will alter their scientific programs to include or preclude the wishes of the people they study. Ethical positions, including positions at either end of the spectrum, have been formulated by individuals and groups, and individuals who do not agree with one group are free to present their own position or form their own group. However, the freedom to choose may be lessening as ethical choices continue to be legislated more and more into requirements. Groups like the American Committee for the Protection of Archaeological Collections (set up to prevent indiscriminate repatriation and/or reburial) can continue to lobby against laws like NAGPRA, but soon, perhaps, writing letters may be all they can do.

SUMMARY

In summary, it has been shown that various subdisciplines of anthropology have lost a portion of their ethical choices to legislative fiat. Prior to the passage of AIRFA (1978), ARPA (1979), the amendments to NHPA (1980, 1992, and 1999), and the passage of NAGPRA (1990), individual archaeologists were able to decide to what extent their personal ethical views influenced their research. Archaeologists who felt that all cultural material within the United States belonged to all of the people of the United States ("cultural patrimony") were able to excavate without having to worry about losing information; consultation was only necessary for scientific, ethnographic, or other analytical reasons.

Individuals who believed that the cultural resources belonged to the ancestors of those who produced them were free to consult closely with traditional or elected officials of Indian tribes that were likely to be related to the "archaeological groups"; if there were competing claims of ancestry, the archaeologist was free to choose which group he or she wished to contact, perhaps the group with which communication was freer or easier.

However, since the passage of the previously mentioned legislative acts, individuals no longer have the same latitude to practice those freedoms. Consultation is now required in the planning stages of a research project since American Indian groups can exert control over tribal lands, allotted lands, and federal lands. Archaeologists must deal with nearly any group that might possibly demonstrate cultural affinity.

If any human remains are recovered, even from private land (since such material may eventually come under the control of a federal agency, federal museum, or a museum that receives federal funding), fewer choices are available to the archaeologist since NAGPRA would apply. Even certain cultural items, if they end up in a museum that receives federal funding, might be returned to an American Indian group.

Is this a bad thing? I do not think so. Archaeologists are aware that we must do all we can to involve local populations in our research, or else archaeology will dwindle until it will be no more than a footnote in history. And in order to involve populations such as American Indian groups, it becomes necessary for archaeology to share the power involved in making decisions that affect the cultural world. The legislative viewpoint outlined in the already mentioned compliance legislation has evolved from that of a Euroamerican one to a more multifaceted perspective on the value and control of the physical and spiritual manifestations of the past.

4

ᴏ～ᴏ⋈ᴏ～ᴏ

Repatriation Legislation

A s discussed in the previous chapter, Congress passed two important pieces of legislation that spell out the rights of tribes to claim human remains and items important to the various tribes. Since the National Museum of the American Indian Act (NMAIA) was the first of the repatriation acts, it will be discussed first, but since the Native American Graves Protection and Repatriation Act (NAGPRA) has had perhaps the most widespread impact on museums and anthropologists, it will be discussed in greater detail.

THE NMAIA AND ITS AMENDMENT

When the 101st U.S. Congress passed the NMAIA (Public Law 101-185) in 1989 establishing the new National Museum of the American Indian, it also required the Smithsonian to inventory, document, and, if requested, repatriate culturally affiliated human remains and funerary objects to federally recognized native groups. In 1996 the NMAIA was amended to add new categories of objects subject to repatriation and to establish deadlines for the distribution of object summaries and inventories of the Smithsonian's collections to the tribes. Definitions of the object categories subject to repatriation generally follow the language of the NAGPRA, which was passed by Congress in 1990.

Object summaries (item by item listings of unassociated funerary objects, sacred objects, and objects of cultural patrimony) were mailed to federally recognized tribes by the end of February 1997. Final inventories of all human remains and associated funerary objects still held by the National Museum of Natural History (NMNH) were mailed on June 1, 1998. Repatriation provisions contained in the NMAIA bring the Smithsonian repatriation legislation into close conformance with deadlines and categories of objects subject to repatriation under NAGPRA.

The NMNH Repatriation Office was established to implement the statutory requirements of the NMAIA and to produce reports that summarize all the available information on the cultural origins of the collections in question. Recommendations for repatriation are made on the basis of this assembled information. Additionally, the Repatriation Office has produced object summaries that identify all ethnological objects in the museum's ethnographic collections associated with particular cultural groups and provide information about how the items were originally acquired. These summaries have been distributed to all federally recognized tribes.

Categories of materials that are eligible for return under the NMAIA include (1) human remains of individuals whose identity is known; (2) culturally affiliated human remains; (3) associated and unassociated funerary objects; (4) sacred objects; and (5) objects of cultural patrimony. In addition, under long-standing museum policy, tribes may request the return of objects transferred to or acquired by the NMNH illegally or under circumstances that render the museum's claim to them invalid.

Culturally affiliated human remains are defined in the legislation as human remains that share a relationship with a present-day Indian tribe that can be demonstrated based on a preponderance of available evidence. Associated and unassociated funerary objects are items that, as part of the death rites of a culture, are believed to have been intentionally placed with an individual of known affiliation at the time of death or later. The only distinction between whether a funerary object is considered unassociated or associated is whether or not the museum has the human remains with which it was originally interred. Sacred objects are specific ceremonial objects that are needed by traditional Native American religious leaders in order to continue practicing their traditional Native American religions by present-day adherents.

Objects of cultural patrimony are more difficult to define and vary among tribes. In general, they are cultural objects that were originally owned by the entire tribe rather than a single individual, and that have an ongoing historical, traditional, or cultural importance to the group. Because the objects were tribally owned rather than individually owned, they cannot have been alienated, appropriated, or conveyed by any individual, at the time they were acquired.

Repatriation of Native American human remains and certain cultural objects may be made by lineal descendants of named individuals, federally recognized Native American tribes, federally recognized Native Alaskan villages, and Native Hawaiian organizations named in the act. Requests from state-recognized Native American tribes are reviewed by the museum on a case-by-case basis.

The NMAIA also required the Smithsonian to establish a special committee to monitor and review the process of inventory, identification, and repatriation. This external review committee consists of seven individuals, four of which must be Native Americans. The review committee may, upon the request of any affected party, review any findings relating to the origin or the return of human remains and cultural objects. They also assist the secretary of the Smithsonian in resolving disputes between groups or between a group and the institution with regard to the disposition of collections that may arise.

THE NAGPRA

Public Law 101-601, the NAGPRA, affirms the rights of lineal descendants, Indian tribes, and Native Hawaiian organizations to custody of Native American human remains, funerary objects, sacred objects, and objects of cultural patrimony.

Signed into law by President George Bush in November 1990, NAGPRA places the responsibility for compliance upon federal agencies and museums that receive federal funds. It required all federal departments, agencies, or instrumentalities of the United States (except for the Smithsonian Institution) to complete summaries and inventories of Native American materials in their control (including those held by nongovernmental repositories) and to ensure compliance regarding inadvertent discoveries and intentional excavations of human remains conducted as part of activities on federal or tribal lands.

A large number of terms and concepts as defined in NAGPRA were used in the 1996 amendment to the NMAIA. The presentation of those definitions again in discussion of NAGPRA seems redundant, but some are included to ensure the terms are understood in relation to the separate laws.

Museums as defined in NAGPRA are more than just places that house artifacts and collections. The definition included any institution or state or local government agency (including any institution of higher learning) that has possession of, or control over, items covered under the act and that receives federal funds. The two important terms, "possession," meaning the physical custody of objects with sufficient legal interest to lawfully treat them as part of the museum's collection, and "control," having a legal interest in objects sufficient to lawfully permit the museum to treat the objects as part of its collection, whether or not the objects are in the physical custody of the museum, were also defined. Generally, a museum that has loaned objects to any entity (individual, museum, or federal agency) is considered to retain control of those objects, although the objects may not be in the physical custody of the museum. Objects in the museum's collection that have been received on loan from another individual, museum, or federal agency are considered to be in the control of the loaning museum.

The act also provided an expanded definition of the phrase "receives Federal funds." As defined in the act, a museum that receives funds from a federal agency through any grant, loan, contract (other than a procurement contract), or arrangement by which a federal agency makes or made available funds to a museum is included. If a larger entity of which the museum is a part receives federal funds (i.e., a university museum where the university receives federal funds), then the museum must comply with NAGPRA regulations. The NAGPRA also applies to certified local governments and tribal museums if they receive federal funds through any grant, loan, or contract. The act does not apply to private individuals and museums that do not receive federal funds or are not part of a larger entity that does receive federal funds.

Under the statute, lineal descendants, Indian tribes, and Native Hawaiian organizations (hereafter, "Indian tribes and Native Hawaiian organizations" will be referred to as "tribal groups" solely for ease of discussion) may claim Native American items covered under the act. While "lineal descendant" is not defined in the statute, the statute makes it clear that lineal descendants have priority over tribal groups in making claims. Regulations require an individual to trace ancestry directly and without interruption by means of a traditional kinship system or by the American colonial law system of descendancy to the Native American individual whose remains, funerary objects, or sacred objects are being claimed. Reference to traditional kinship systems is designed to accommodate various systems that Indian tribes might use to reckon kinship. "Indian tribe" is defined to mean any tribe, band, nation, or other organized Indian group or community of Indians, including any Native Alaskan village, as defined in or established by the Alaska Native Claims Settlement Act (43 U.S.C. 1601 et seq.), that is recognized as eligible for the special programs and services provided by the United States to Indians because of their status as Indians. This definition was drawn explicitly from the American Indian Self Determination and Education Act (25 U.S.C. 450b). Only federally recognized Indian groups have standing to make a direct claim under the act.

The statute defines "Native Hawaiian organization" as any organization that serves and represents the interests of Native Hawaiians, has as a primary and stated purpose the provision of services to Native Hawaiians, and has expertise in Native Hawaiian affairs. The statute specifically identifies the Office of Hawaiian Affairs and Hui Malama I Na Kupuna 'O Hawai'i Nei as being Native Hawaiian organizations.

The NAGPRA affects four types of Native American cultural items held in museums: human remains, funerary objects, sacred objects, and objects of cultural patrimony. Note that the term "Native American" (meaning "of, or relating to, a tribe, people, or culture indigenous to the United States including Alaska and Hawaii") is used only to refer to items covered under the act, and is never used in the statute or regulations in reference to any living individual or group of individuals.

"Human remains" (the physical remains of a person) has been interpreted broadly to include bones, teeth, hair, ashes, or mummified or otherwise preserved soft tissues, but does not include remains or portions of remains freely given or naturally shed by the individual (such as hair made into ropes or nets). The act makes no distinction between fully articulated burials and isolated bones and teeth, but it does consider human remains incorporated into funerary objects, sacred objects, or objects of cultural patrimony as part of that object.

"Funerary items" are items that are reasonably believed to have been placed intentionally at the time of death or later with or near individual human remains. They must be defined by the preponderance of the evidence as having been removed from a specific burial site of an individual affiliated with a particular tribal group, or as being related to specific individuals or families or to known human remains. "Burial Site" means any natural or prepared physical location (whether below, on, or above the surface of the earth) into which individual human remains were deposited as part of the death rite or ceremony of a culture. Rock cairns or pyres are also considered to be burial sites. Items that inadvertently come into contact with human remains are not considered funerary objects, but objects that are intentionally placed near, but not necessarily with, the human remains at the time of death or later are considered to be funerary objects. The act distinguishes between associated funerary objects and unassociated funerary objects based solely upon whether or not the human remains with which the objects are associated are in the possession or control of the museum or federal agency.

"Sacred objects" are defined as specific ceremonial objects needed by traditional tribal religious leaders for the practice of traditional tribal religions by present-day adherents. "Traditional religious leaders" are further defined by the statute. While many items might be imbued with sacredness in the eyes of an individual, NAGPRA regulations are specifically limited to objects that were devoted to a traditional tribal religious ceremony or ritual and that have religious significance or function in the continued observance or renewal of such ceremony.

"Objects of cultural patrimony" are defined as items having ongoing historical, traditional, or cultural importance central to the tribal group itself, rather than property owned by an individual tribal member. They are considered to be items of such central importance to a tribal group that they could not have been given away or sold by any individual tribal member, even though an individual tribal member or family usually might maintain day-to-day care of it. An additional requirement is that they also must have been considered inalienable by the Indian tribe at the time the object was separated from the group. Objects of cultural patrimony include items such as the Zuni war gods and the Confederacy wampum belts of the Onondaga.

The statute lays out a mechanism for federal land managers, museums, and agency officials to consult with lineal descendants and tribal groups and reach a determination regarding the proper disposition of objects covered under the act that might be excavated or discovered on federal or tribal lands. The processes for dealing with excavations or discoveries on federal or tribal lands are different than those for dealing with the disposition of objects within museum or federal agency collections.

Provisions relating to intentional excavations and inadvertent discoveries on federal and tribal lands (but not to private or state lands) went into effect on November 16, 1990. These provisions were designed to help in the proper disposition of items covered under the act that might be intentionally excavated or inadvertently discovered on federal or tribal lands.

"Intentional excavations" are the planned archaeological removal of items covered under the act that are found under or on the surface of federal or tribal lands, and, under these provisions, federal officials are required to take steps to determine whether a planned activity may result in the excavation of items covered under the act. Any items covered under the act that might be recovered must be excavated in accordance with the requirements of the Archaeological Resources Protection Act (ARPA) and its implementing regulations, and only after consultation with the appropriate tribal group. Intentional excavation of items covered under the act on tribal lands can only proceed with the consent of the appropriate tribal group. The procedures require written proof that consultation has occurred before the responsible agency official may issue required permits.

An "inadvertent discovery"—an unanticipated encounter or detection of items covered under the act found under or on the surface of federal or tribal lands—requires immediate telephone no-tification, with written confirmation, to the responsible federal agency official. Inadvertent discoveries on tribal lands must be re-ported immediately to the responsible Indian tribal official. If the inadvertent discovery occurs in connection with an ongoing activ-ity, the activity must stop in the area of the inadvertent discovery and a reasonable effort made to protect the items covered under the act. Notification and consultation with the appropriate tribal group about the disposition of the items covered under the act must be done as soon as possible (but no later than three working days af-ter receipt of the written confirmation of notification) by the respon-sible agency official. The activity may resume thirty days after cer-tification by the notified federal agency of receipt of the written confirmation of notification. The activity may also resume at any time after a written, binding agreement is executed between the federal agency and the affiliated tribal group(s) that adopt a recov-ery plan for the excavation or removal of the items covered under the act.

Once the group that appears to be entitled to custody of the ma-terials is determined, the federal agency official must publish a general notice of the proposed disposition in a newspaper of gen-eral circulation in the area where the materials were excavated or discovered and, if applicable, in a newspaper of general circulation in the area in which the affiliated tribal group's members now re-side. Transfer of the materials cannot take place until at least thirty days after the publication of the notice in order to allow time for any additional claimants to come forward.

The statute also requires museums and federal agencies to inform tribal groups of items covered under the act that are within their collections through either summaries or inventories.

"Summaries" are defined as written descriptions of collections that may contain unassociated funerary objects, sacred objects, or objects of cultural patrimony and are to have been completed by November 16, 1993. They were basically a simple notification to each tribal group of the nature of the collections held by the mu-seum or federal agency relating to that group. The summary was intended as a initial step to bring tribal groups, tribal representa-tives, and traditional religious leaders into consultation with a museum or federal agency in order to help in the identification of specific unassociated funerary objects, sacred objects, or objects of cultural patrimony.

"Inventories" are much more detailed descriptions of materials within a museum's collections. These item-by-item descriptions of human remains and associated funerary objects must be completed in consultation with tribal groups and represent a decision by the museum or federal official about the cultural affiliation of particular human remains or associated funerary objects. Inventories are to have been completed by November 16, 1995, but some museums have been granted time extensions by the Interior Department based on their "good faith effort" to have completed the requisite inventories.

Inventories of "culturally unidentifiable human remains"—human remains for which no lineal descendant or culturally affiliated tribal group can be determined—are provided by the departmental consulting archaeologist to the NAGPRA Review Committee, a group of seven private citizens charged with making recommendations concerning any questions regarding the implementation of NAGPRA regulations and the disposition of these remains.

The system outlined by the statute provides a framework for resolving issues surrounding the disposition of Native American human remains, funerary objects, sacred objects, and objects of cultural patrimony excavated or discovered on federal or tribal lands or held in federal or museum collections. The regulations, while wordy and somewhat filled with "bureaucrat-ese," provide a first step in institutionalizing consultation with tribal groups about human remains and objects of continuing cultural importance.

THE LEGAL IMPLICATIONS OF REPATRIATION

American Indian groups hailed the passage of NAGPRA as an opportunity to right centuries-old wrongs perpetrated against American Indian graves. In a symposium sponsored by the *Arizona State Law Journal*, many authors discussed the "new" law as it impacted various institutions that dealt with Native American human remains and cultural material.

While archaeology was not the only culprit to have used American Indian human remains as study objects—"Human remains were obtained by soldiers, government agents, pothunters, private citizens, museum collecting crews, and scientists in the name of profit, entertainment, science, or development" (Trope and Echo-Hawk 1992: 40)—it was perhaps the most visible.

As James Riding In wrote:

> Individuals who violate the sanctity of the grave outside of the law are viewed as criminals, Satan worshippers, or imbalanced. When caught, tried, and convicted, the guilty are usually incarcerated, fined, or placed in mental institutions. Yet public opinion and legal loopholes have until recently enabled white society to loot and pillage with impunity American Indian cemeteries. Archaeology, a branch of anthropology that still attempts to sanctify this tradition of exploiting dead Indians, arose as an honorable profession from this sacrilege. (1992: 12)

But NAGPRA was neither written to impede scientific progress nor to provide American Indian groups special status under the federal legal system. In discussing the legislative history of the law, Jack F. Trope and Walter Echo-Hawk note, "NAGPRA is, first and foremost, human rights legislation . . . designed to address the flagrant violation of the 'civil rights of America's first citizens'" (1992: 59).

Additionally, Maricopa County Superior Court judge Sherry Hutt sees NAGPRA as a law that will "strengthen federal prosecutors' ability to protect Native American graves and cultural treasures by hampering the profit incentive" (1992: 135), the same thing federal and local archaeologists had attempted to do regularly through education and legislation.

THE SCIENTIFIC RESPONSE TO NAGPRA

A more complete discussion of the scientific response to the repatriation legislation is provided in chapter 2, but, needless to say, it ranged from complete support to total opposition. While no archaeological organization supported the initial repatriation legislation, nationwide organizations became deeply involved in the lobbying efforts to ensure that the final version of the NAGPRA was indeed a compromise between American Indian wishes and those of the archaeological communities of the United States.

Larry Zimmerman (1997) provides a good summary of the repatriation issues as they have impacted the discipline of archaeology. His article discusses the four stages that archaeology went through in dealing with repatriation: denial, dialogue, analysis, and compromise.

In the denial phase, argues Zimmerman, the discipline challenged Indian claims, rationalizing, as he writes, that "academic freedom has precedence and that the remains are the heritage of all cultures" (1997: 93). This stance, that the goals of science as a worldwide, humanist pursuit are somehow more important than the wishes of individual cultures, is still heard as an excuse for the unfettered practice of archaeological excavations in societies throughout the world (see Gough 1996; Meighan 1992; Mulvaney 1991).

During the dialogue phase, Zimmerman notes that, while not all archaeologists agreed that problems existed, the discipline began a series of dialogues to gain an understanding of the Indian perceptions of the problems. It is interesting to note that archaeologists continue to court dialogues.

Zimmerman's third phase, analysis, came about as "some anthropologists became curious about why the controversy arose and why it continued. The issue itself became a matter of intellectual investigation" (1997: 101). Anthropologists began to study the processes that evolved along with the changing relationships between anthropologists and indigenous populations.

Zimmerman's last phase, compromise, provides a brief listing of some "historical" (if the late 1960s might be considered historic) compromises made between American Indians and archaeologists. It also provides a glimpse of the reasoning behind American Indian attempts at getting national repatriation laws passed rather than state or local laws (1997: 105).

NAGPRA falls heavily on those individuals who analyze and interpret the human remains subject to repatriation as well as on those who initially encounter those remains. In articles such as "Human Skeletal Remains: Preservation or Reburial?" (Ubelaker and Grant 1989: 249–87), "Why Anthropologists Study Human Remains" (Landau and Steele 1996: 209–28), and "NAGPRA Is Forever: Osteology and the Repatriation of Skeletons" (Rose, Green, and Green 1996: 81–103), biological anthropologists and osteologists outline the types of information that result from the study of human remains. Although these might be construed to be nothing more than a justification for the continued study of human remains, they nonetheless offer an attempt to educate not only American Indians but also other anthropologists about the uses of osteology in the gathering of information concerning life styles of human beings.

AMBIGUITIES AND INADEQUACIES OF NAGPRA

The passage of NAGPRA gave American Indians some of the tools necessary to implement the changes they had protested for in the 1970s. Many authors (Hutt 1992; Hutt, Jones, and McAllister 1992; Tsosie 1997; Welsh 1992), believe that NAGPRA is human rights legislation aimed at providing equal treatment to all human remains under the law, without consideration of "race" or cultural background. The law, they believe, was meant to remedy the unequal treatment of American Indian remains by previous generations of American military, bureaucrats, and scientists. But with the law's passage, tribal groups quickly realized it was not the panacea they hoped it would be, and Indians quickly spoke out on the inadequacies and ambiguities of NAGPRA.

American Indians complained that scientists were using the inventories and summaries required of museums in Section 5, subsection (a) of NAGPRA for additional scientific data collection under the guise of complying with NAGPRA. While the law does not authorize the initiation of new scientific studies, it does not preclude it when the museum deems it necessary for determining the cultural affiliation of a set of human remains (Section5[b][2]), or when the materials are "indispensable for completion of a specific scientific study, the outcome of which would be of major benefit to the United States" (Section 7[b]).

In the 1995 oversight hearing on the implementation of NAGPRA, Kunani Nihipali, a leader of Hui Malama I Na Kapuna 'O Hawai'i Nei, a Native Hawaiian organization, called for a clarification of the role of scientific study, asking that "where existing documentation establishes geographic location and cultural affiliation by clear, reasonable belief, or the preponderance standard of evidence, scientific studies of any kind on ancestral skeletal material remains [be] prohibited" (Superintendent of Documents 1996: 158).

Other tribes were concerned about the apparent authorization of study prior to repatriation of materials allowed in Section 7 of NAGPRA. At the same oversight hearing, Jesse Taken Alive, chairman of the Standing Rock Sioux Tribe, noted:

> It was only when Native people . . . rose to stop the racist practice of the robbery and study of our graves was the "loss" to science loudly and arrogantly lamented. Amid great gnashing of teeth, *the rush was on* to study, document, analyze, and further desecrate our relatives before the precious "scientific and cultural materials" could be "destroyed" through reburial.
>
> *In our view, the science and museum industries have only themselves to blame that they did not correctly catalog and store our dead relatives while they had them, and should not now be allowed to gather one more iota of data from our relatives under the cloak of NAGPRA.* (Superintendent of Documents 1996: 231, emphasis in original)

Scientists might argue that since the deadlines for inventorying and summarizing museum collections have past such arguments are moot, but the scientific study of American Indian human remains is still a valid concern.

Additionally, many American Indian groups cannot understand why the graves protection portion of NAGPRA was not applied to all lands within the United States, rather than just to federal or tribal lands, since the entire continent was at one time Indian land. The National Congress of American Indians, the oldest and largest national organization representing American Indians called for "amendatory language to the NAGPRA to extend protection of funerary remains and objects on all lands within the exterior boundaries of the United States wherever they may be situated" (NCAI Resolution No. NV-93-170). NAGPRA Review Committee chairwoman Tessie Naranjo of Santa Clara Pueblo noted that the NAGRRA Review Committee itself experienced frustration over this issue (Superintendent of Documents 1996: 149).

In a review of the legislative history of NAGPRA, Trope and Echo-Hawk noted that thirty-four states had enacted burial protection laws that "typically prohibit intentional disturbance of unmarked graves, provide guidelines to protect the graves, and mandate disposition of human remains from the graves in a way that guarantees reburial after a period of study" (1992: 52). They also noted the constitutionality of the laws had been upheld, citing as examples cases in California, Minnesota, and Oregon (53).

Why is such extension of NAGPRA important? According to Melinda Zeder's survey of American archaeologists, approximately 49 percent of archaeologists worked either within the government (23 percent), the private sector (18 percent), or within a museum setting (8 percent) (1997: 47). Although these figures might vary from the true proportions of archaeologists employed in these areas, Zeder feels they are a good fit to the actual makeup of American archaeology (48).

If one assumes that private sector and museum archaeologists are as closely tied to federal regulations as their government counterparts, only about one-half of American archaeologists are bound by the NAGPRA or the NMAIA. Academic archaeologists, those more often participating in "pure research," are less confined by federal regulations and made up 35 percent of the survey population. When these archaeologists conduct research on federal or tribal lands, their research is covered under NAGPRA, as are the artifacts that they collect. However, if their research is conducted on private land, they are less restrained. While the artifacts might eventually come under control of NAGPRA (if the museums where the artifacts are curated receive federal funds), their initial excavations may not be as stringently controlled.

The ascription of property rights to archaeological resources is, as Ruthann Knudson notes, "a complicated legal, as well as social, issue" (1991: 4). While human remains may be protected under various state laws, federal intervention on private land is sometimes seen as a violation of the "takings clause" of the U.S. Constitution if the landowner is somehow denied access or free use of his or her property without adequate compensation.

Another point of concern to American Indians is in relation to American Indian human remains and funerary objects whose cultural affiliation has not been established.

At the 1995 oversight hearing on the implementation of NAGPRA, Cecil Antone, lieutenant governor of the Gila River Indian Community at Sacaton, Arizona, noted that "Even though they are not identified [as to culture], they are human beings. They were human beings" (Superintendent of Documents 1996: 37). Jesse Taken Alive of the Standing Rock Sioux Tribe said the tribe believes "those remains dating back 500 years or more are American Indians. . . . Give them back to the people and let us decide how that should be done, because, after all, as American Indians, as indigenous people, those are our ancestors" (Superintendent of Documents 1996: 42).

Even the NAGPRA Review Committee felt this issue was a point of frustration. Dan Monroe, a member of the committee in 1996, noted in testimony at the oversight hearing that *"the controversy is hottest in respect to disposition of ancient Native American remains . . . [that] can seldom be affiliated with a specific tribe. . . . Native Americans almost unanimously argue that they are culturally and otherwise affiliated with these remains and that their religious and cultural beliefs dictate that the remains be returned and reburied"* (Superintendent of Documents 1996: 125, emphasis in original).

In 1998, the NAGPRA Review Committee issued a set of Draft Principles of Agreement Regarding the Disposition of Culturally Unidentifiable Human Remains. These principles presented guidelines for the ultimate disposition of these types of remains. While no specific remedies are defined for every case, they do offer suggestions for disposition in cases where the human remains are associated with a nonfederally recognized tribe, suggest regional consultations where such approaches would prove beneficial, and for situations where the human remains represent a population for which there are no present-day cultural survivors.

American Indian views on the issue of repatriating human remains and other items to nonfederally recognized tribes are divided, but for differing reasons. Many tribes feel that nonfederally recognized American Indian tribes are no less Indian than their federally recognized counterparts, while others are afraid that to allow standing under NAGPRA would allow such groups to bypass the normally tedious process of federal recognition.

Again, Tessie Naranjo, former chair of the NAGPRA Review Committee, noted at the 1995 oversight hearing that Congress needed to find a way to "permit Native American groups not presently recognized by . . . the BIA to repatriate their human remains, funerary objects, sacred objects, or objects of cultural patrimony" (Superintendent of Documents 1996: 22). Additionally, testimony provided by the Keepers of the Treasures-Alaska also called for such congressional action. In the words of an Alaska elder: "'it didn't matter . . . when the human remains of nonfederally recognized Indian tribes were taken . . . it irks me that living human beings are technically not in existence merely because the U.S. Government does not recognize them'" (Superintendent of Documents 1996: 72). Additionally, Duane Champagne, director of the American Indian Studies Center at the University of California at Los Angeles provided a five-page letter noting the problems with such a policy in California alone (Superintendent of Documents 1996: 99–103).

While all tribes agree that human remains of unrecognized American Indian groups have been and always will be American Indian, many are concerned about extending rights to all groups under NAGPRA. In a statement prepared for the March 1997 NAGPRA Review Committee meeting in Oklahoma, seven tribes from southwestern Oklahoma—the Apache Tribe of Oklahoma, the Caddo Tribe, the Comanche Tribe, the Delaware Tribe of Western Oklahoma, the Fort Sill Apache Tribe, the Kiowa Tribe, and the Wichita and Affiliated Tribes—felt repatriation should occur only to federally recognized groups. While they felt that human remains, regardless of affiliation, should not be left in museums, they expressed a concern that to repatriate human remains to nonfederally recognized tribes could potentially assign rights and authority to groups that have come into existence without a legitimate claim of continuity. The working group feels that culturally unidentifiable human remains should be repatriated to the federally recognized tribes on whose aboriginal lands the remains were found, with the review committee making decisions in cases of multiple tribes claiming the same ancestral lands.

As a final example of the inadequacies of NAGPRA, under 3(c) and (d), the excavation of American Indian human remains and objects must follow the Archaeological Resources Protection Act of 1979. But what happens if a tribal group does not want the items excavated? If the tribe has the permitting authority for the land where the remains are located, the tribe may refuse to issue an antiquities permit and thereby prevent excavation, but, absent the tribe's permitting authority, the law requires only that consultation occur, not that tribal permission be granted. Additionally, if the tribes will have the right of ownership and control as called for under 3(c)(3), it creates a situation where the artifacts magically become tribal property only *after* the scientist is finished removing and/or studying them, but not before.

And the situation gets dicey in the case of an inadvertent discovery situation on federal land if there are no known or easily discovered lineal descendants. If the material cannot be reasonably identified to tribe, then the material becomes the "property" of the tribe that has the closest cultural affiliation with the material and that states a claim for it. Of course, this might require scientific study of the material to determine which group might have the "closest" affiliation, something many tribes do not want.

And if the material cannot be identified as to cultural affiliation? If the materials are found on federal land that is recognized by a final judgment of the Indian Claims Commission or the U.S. Court of Claims as the aboriginal land of some Indian tribe, then the material goes to the tribe that is recognized as the aboriginal occupant of the land, or to another tribe if it can demonstrate a stronger cultural affiliation than the aboriginal occupant of the land on which the materials were found.

Ultimately, it can happen that no tribe may be judged to be an aboriginal occupant of the land or that no tribe will be viewed as being culturally affiliated with the materials, something that can definitely create difficulty in getting the remains repatriated in an efficient manner.

SUMMARY

The passage of the NMAIA and the NAGPRA forced the discipline of archaeology to react more strongly than necessary. While the importance of human remains in the study of past diets, lifeways, and cultures has been recognized by various authors, archaeology nonetheless failed to make clear the objectives of wishing to retain control over human remains and cultural objects encountered within excavations.

The impact of the laws' requirements was immediately felt by those museums that were required to prepare inventories of the human remains and associated grave goods, sacred items, and items of cultural patrimony within their collections. The inventories were then forwarded to American Indian groups that were often forced to wade through computer generated listings in an effort to discover those items for which they had an interest. The sudden influx of such lists strained programs, many of which were already underfunded, and forced some tribal programs to either curtail aspects of their cultural resource programs or to try to come to grips with the mountain of data with which they did not know what to do.

Archaeologists and organizations were quick to recognize the problems involved in consultation and repatriation of material recovered or donated before the current legislative controls. However, legal analyses of NAGPRA pointed out that archaeologists were not entitled to "own" the materials that the tribes were requesting, and that the control of such objects covered under the law was vested in the tribes or in members of the tribes.

While museum officials and curators might have been concerned with the loss of items within their collections, archaeologists appeared to be more concerned with the freedom to pursue "science" and the academic quest for answers to questions about which most American Indians might not care. Additionally, as is the case in the Kennewick situation, anthropologists soon entered into the legal arena in a fight to retain the right to attempt to answer questions that influence the worldwide knowledge base.

But not all American Indians are against the practice of archaeology, and some tribes have developed programs that utilize archaeology on the reservations and other lands under their control. The following chapters provide some case studies that illustrate the variation in tribal involvement with the discipline of archaeology within their areas of influence.

5

⌒⌒○◄○⌒○

Sampling the Attitudes
of Archaeologists

The breakdown of virulent racism in the twentieth century has
enabled Indians to challenge with a remarkable degree of success the practices of archaeologists and other grave looters.
(Riding In 1992: 12)

Representatives of indigenous populations often perceive archaeologists as people who dig up the cultural and human remains
of minority populations out of an inherently racist attitude of the
sort suggested by James Riding In. While archaeology might have
grown from a colonial racism of the sort decried by Riding In, archaeologists have less freedom today concerning the types of actions in which they might engage than they did thirty years ago.

Having been involved in the federal compliance system in one
aspect or another during the past twenty years, I cannot recall meeting that many insensitive, neocolonialist archaeologists who gave
no consideration of the wishes of the descendants of a site's original inhabitants. I have met some, I hate to admit, but there are fewer
of those now than before.

Thus, since American Indians and even some archaeologists cast
a blanket of cultural insensitivity over all archaeologists, I became
curious about the extent that certain variables might influence an
archaeologist's decisions to conduct excavations.

For example, as a review of the previous chapters on federal legislation and repatriation indicates, the primary variable that influences government involvement in cultural resources is landownership. Melinda Zeder's census of American archaeologists noted that approximately 49 percent of 1,364 archaeologists who responded to a questionnaire were employed either in the government sector (23 percent), the museum sector (8 percent), or the private sector (18 percent), and only 35 percent in the academic sector. The remaining 16 percent of the respondents were employed in other, less well-defined categories (1997: 46–47). While Zeder recognizes that the census figures might vary from the true proportions of archaeologists employed in such areas, she feels they are a good fit to the actual makeup of American archaeology (48).

If one assumes that archaeologists employed in government, museum, and private sectors are restrained by federal regulations such as NAGPRA and the National Historic Preservation Act, then at least 49 percent of American archaeologists are controlled by restrictions that govern major portions of their research. While archaeologists employed in the academic sector—who are not a part of a university Cultural Resources Management (CRM) program—might be less confined by federal regulations, they are currently experiencing more federal restrictions on their research (i.e., when collections obtained from a privately funded excavation are curated in museums that receive federal funds, they become subject to repatriation under NAGPRA).

Additionally, as a part of the NAGPRA consultation process, an archaeologist must take into consideration the wishes of a descendant group before beginning the scientific examination of a site. And, to archaeologists, the presence of an ethnographic record of a tribal group's preferences toward cultural and human remains gives additional weight to their wishes.

In 1991, I began a research project aimed at understanding individual archaeologist's views about issues affecting American Indian concerns (Watkins 1994). I developed a questionnaire that presented a series of scenarios that required the responding archaeologist to react to circumstances and then to answer questions based on their interpretation of the situation. Statistical analyses performed on the database formed by the individual responses were used to help interpret whether and to what extent variables influenced the respondents' actions.

General publications, such as *Approaches to Developing Question-naires* (De Maio 1983) and *Survey Research Methods* (Fowler 1984), were used to get a general background into the formulation of questionnaires and to gain tools for developing questions, procedures for testing the questionnaire draft, and techniques for evaluating the questionnaire. It was decided that an anonymous questionnaire provided the most unbiased means of collecting the data necessary for the research, since it was likely that archaeologists would respond more candidly to situations if personal recognition was neither necessary nor possible.

Copies of the questionnaire were distributed at five conferences as well as mailed to the state archaeologists' offices throughout the United States. Four hundred questionnaires were distributed at the November 1991 Plains Anthropological Conference in Lawrence, Kansas; seventy-five at the March 1992 Caddo Conference in Shreveport, Louisiana; two hundred at the January 1993 Society for Historical Archaeology/Council on Underwater Archaeology meeting in Kansas City, Missouri; and seventy-five at the 1993 Caddo Conference in Norman, Oklahoma. Two hundred fifty questionnaires were mailed to state archaeologists' offices in the United States (five to each office), and fifty questionnaires were distributed to anthropologists and anthropology students at the University of Oklahoma campus and included in the Plains Conference totals. Of the thousand questionnaires distributed, 191 were returned and form the database for this analysis.

The conferences that were chosen for the distribution of the questionnaires were done so because of their historical relationship with American Indian groups at the time of the research as a means of getting a cross-section of anthropological thought regarding American Indian issues. For example, anthropologists associated with the Caddo Conference have strong interactions with members of the Caddo Tribe and are aware of American Indian thoughts concerning cultural resources in the Caddo archaeological/anthropological sphere. Anthropologists associated with the Plains Anthropological Conference may be generally less involved with American Indian issues than those from the Caddo conference, although their research does involve them with American Indian issues, and their interactions are increasing. The individuals who provided information from the Society for Historic Archaeology/Conference on Underwater Archaeology meetings are probably least affected by

American Indian concerns than the others, but they provide a different viewpoint on the situations involving non-Indian material.

Finally, the questionnaires obtained from the mailing to the offices of the state historic preservation officers appear more influenced by the federal legislation that such individuals are forced to deal with on a daily basis. However, those who received the questionnaire were asked to fill one out and to forward the remainders to people within their office *or* others within the state who they thought would respond. It is therefore difficult to categorize the responders from this group.

The use of focused scenarios or "vignettes" in survey research is not new. T. A. Nosanchuk suggested that they force the respondents to function like informants, "they first read the vignette and then answer questions which require them to make inferences" (1970: 108). Cheryl Alexander and Henry Becker went even further, writing

> A major problem in public opinion and survey research is the ambiguity that often arises when survey respondents are asked to make decisions and judgments from rather abstract and limited information. The use of vignettes helps to standardize the social stimulus across respondents and at the same time makes the decision-making situation more real. (1978: 103)

RESPONSE POPULATION

Population data for the respondents were collected as part of this research project to gain an understanding for the body of archaeologists who responded to this survey instrument. It is unfortunate that I was unaware of a large-scale survey being done by the Society for American Archaeology in 1993–1994, which resulted in *The American Archaeologist: A Profile* (Zeder 1997). Had I chosen the same categories in certain response fields, the data between Zeder's survey and this would be more comparable. However, throughout the general population section of the chapter, I will attempt to show comparisons of questionnaire data to that of Zeder.

Certain questions in the questionnaire ask the respondent to describe age, highest academic degree attained, years of experience in the discipline (including time spent in school), and a self-definition of professional status. Also requested was a self-definition of the respondent's minority status and classification, if any.

Of the responders to Zeder's survey, 122 had terminal bachelor's degrees, 439 had terminal master's degrees, and 845 had doctorates (1997: 21–22). However, Zeder's data measures only the terminal degrees of nonstudent (i.e., "professional") members of the SAA. Of those who responded to the research questionnaire, nineteen were still working on their bachelor's degree; eighteen had completed a bachelor's degree in what they identified as their terminal degree; sixteen were pursuing their master's degree; forty-eight had a terminal master's degree; sixteen had a master's degree and were pursuing their doctorate; fifteen were all but dissertation; and fifty-nine had their doctorate. In Zeder's terms, of the responders to this questionnaire, eighteen had a terminal bachelor's degree, forty-eight had a terminal master's degree, and fifty-nine had a doctorate.

Comparisons between Zeder's survey and this questionnaire show that the people with a Ph.D. in the Zeder survey make up 60 percent of the responding "professional" population, while they form less that half (47 percent) of those who responded to this research questionnaire.

In relation to the ages of the responders, again the data were collected in different categories. In my questionnaire data, the age categories end at the decade (i.e., twenty-one to thirty years of age), while Zeder's begin with the decade (i.e., twenty to twenty-nine), making comparisons tenuous. Assuming that the decade errors (misplacement of actual responders on either end of the decade) is consistent, a comparison of Zeder's student and professional categories and this data (table 5.1) would look like this:

Table 5.1   Age Distribution of Respondants

Age Group	Zeder (%)	Watkins (%)
<30	101 (6)	20 (10)
31–40	384 (23)	65 (34)
41–50	712 (44)	89 (47)
51–60	280 (17)	15 (8)
60+	157 (10)	2 (1)

It is difficult to compare the employment categories used in this questionnaire as opposed to Zeder's. A glance at the following table reveals that the categories chosen overlap to some extent Zeder's classes, although there may be too many assumptions to try to force the categories to merge. Suffice it to say, based on the responses received, fifty-four archaeologists had jobs related to academic pursuits in a college or university (roughly comparable to Zeder's "academic" category), eighty-eight had governmental employment positions (roughly comparable to Zeder's "government"), and twenty-eight were in private positions. That leaves twenty in the "other" category, and one "no response." Unfortunately, in the questionnaire I submitted, there was no "museum" category.

If we compare just the three roughly equivalent categories (table 5.2), it appears thus:

Table 5.2   Employment Category of Respondants

Age Group	Zeder (%)	Watkins (%)
Academic	477 (35)	54 (28)
Government	314 (23)	88 (46)
Private	246 (18)	28 (15)
Other	327 (24)	21 (11)

*Zeder's actual counts are not given; N is derived by mulitplying the total given by category percentages.

Finally, when the respondents to my research were asked if they considered themselves to be members of a minority group, twelve answered "yes" and listed "women" as their minority; four listed themselves as "Native American"; one responded "African American"; and two responded "Hispanic." One responded "Croatian," and two other individuals responded they were minorities but did not specify. The rest did not consider themselves to be minorities (including one who was one-sixty-fourth Native American by blood and another who was one-eight Abnaki—an Eastern Algonkin group).

It is not surprising that the characteristics of the Zeder survey population and the questionnaire population samples are different. The population data between the two surveys are not really comparable. Zeder's survey instrument was mailed to the membership of the SAA under the sponsorship of the SAA, while the questionnaire was almost totally opportunistic in that mostly it was distributed at archaeological conferences. Even mailing the questionnaire to the offices of the state archaeologists did not ensure that any particular age, education, or employment category was represented.

SCENARIOS USED IN THE RESEARCH

While the original questionnaire presented the reader six scenarios (Watkins 1994, appendix A), some drawing upon situations introduced in previous scenarios, this research focused only on the responses to specific questions in two scenarios, renumbered I and II (figs. 5.1 and 5.2). The first scenario sets the stage for the next one, which references and alters the already presented situation. A set of questions based on each scenario then asks for the reader's opinion.

I used two nonparametric statistics to test for significance: Spearman's *r* statistic and Friedman's chi-square statistic. Spearman's *r* statistic (r_s) is based on relative rankings of information, equivalent to computing a Pearson correlation on ranked data rather than on raw data. Friedman's chi-square was used to test whether the response distribution changes resulting from altering the situations were statistically significant. Since the changes to the situations deal primarily with a single variable, the comparison of the responses to the two questions may be considered an analysis of "repeated measures," with the first question under consideration acting as the "before measure," and the second serving the function of the "after measure." The hypotheses for the test is

H_0: There is no difference in mean ranks between repeated measures.

H_a: There is a difference in mean ranks between repeated measures.

ROLE OF LANDOWNERSHIP

Individual archaeologists were asked to respond to certain situations that hinged on landownership. I assumed that their responses would almost certainly be based on the situations that arose; if the land were owned by a private individual, control of artifacts and landowner wishes would appear to carry more influence than if the land were publicly or tribally owned. If the land were federally controlled, the archaeologist's personal choices would be lessened because of legislative controls.

Private ownership carries more ethical problems, because the freedoms of scientific and humanistic choices are less rigidly defined. The scientist must decide which group has a stronger claim, whether the good of science (knowledge) outweighs the good of the tribal people (humanity), and the extent the tribal population should be involved in the cultural resource decisions.

Private ownership, however, does not preclude the pressure subjected to a researcher. The situation at the East Wenatchee Clovis Site in Washington State (as described in chapter 8) is a perfect example, for members of the Colville Confederated Tribes brought tremendous pressure to bear against the investigator, ultimately influencing the amount of work undertaken. The very fact that a state archaeological permit was required before the archaeologists could excavate a site on private property is noteworthy. The exertion of state control over private property is rare, especially in relation to cultural resources.

While scenario I is presented in its entirety in figure 5.1, a brief discussion highlights the important portions. The scenario begins with the discovery of graves on private land, graves related to an 1876 battle between the U.S. Army and the Hakawi Indians. The Hakawi are opposed to excavations, but the army wants its men reburied in the National Cemetery at Arlington and there is no way to distinguish the occupants of the graves without excavation and study of the human remains within the graves. Do you excavate?

The responses to the initial situation depicted in row I1 of table 5.3 are generally evenly distributed, although there is a slight skew against excavation, with seven more people choosing the "strongly disagree" response. Actual counts are presented in table 5.3.

The general influence of landownership in archaeologists' attitudes about excavation can be gleaned by comparing responses to questions 3 and 4 of the scenario. Question 3 adds the support of the soldiers' descendants for excavation, while maintaining the land in private ownership, but with continued Hakawi opposition to excavation. Question 4, however, while maintaining the soldiers' descendants' support, changes the landownership to the Hakawi. If the Friedman's chi-square analysis of the repeated measures is

Figure 5.1   Scenario I Used in the Research

Scenario I Conflict on Private Property

A project, on private land, has encountered what appears to be carefully constructed graves. Stains appearing on the freshly scraped surface of a proposed well pad are identical to those known to have contained Hakawi burials. The location is identical to one recorded as the site of the military encounter between the Hakawi and the U.S. Army in 1876 that you recently discovered mentioned in the Military Archives.

The story, by a Private Jones, recounted how a group of Hakawi and the army had met in a narrow pass and battled. The Hakawi prevailed, killing everyone in the party but he, although sustaining a major loss of life themselves. The only reason his life was spared, he said, was because he fought so hard and bravely. He also recalled how, when the battle was over, he and the surviving Hakawi "ceremoniously buried the warriors, but left to the vermin the cowards" (including, he noted, some from both sides). He had been unable to recall the location of the battle.

All other records of the battle were lost, including the names of the troops lost in the battle. Private Jones's account of the burying party also brought out the fact that all of the men were totally stripped prior to burial, "so that their earthly possessions would not pollute their final resting place." Therefore, the identity of the human remains in each of the graves can only be determined by scientific study of the bones themselves.

The Hakawi are vehement against the distrubance of their warriors. The army is delighted to have found its lost men, and wishes to have them returned for ceremonial reburial in the National Cemetery in Arlington. One is also destined for the Tomb of the Unknown Soldier, with associated fanfare.

1. Excavations should be undertaken.

Strongly Agree / Agree / Neither Agree nor Disagree / Disagree / Strongly Disagree

2. The names of the dead soldiers are known, and their descendants do not wish the remains disturbed. Excavations should be undertaken.

Strongly Agree / Agree / Neither Agree nor Disagree / Disagree / Strongly Disagree

3. The descendants of the soldiers (as a group) want the remains shipped to Arlington. Excavations should be undertaken.

Strongly Agree / Agree / Neither Agree nor Disagree / Disagree / Strongly Disagree

4. The remains are on Hakawi land, under the same circumstances. Excavations should be undertaken.

Strongly Agree / Agree / Neither Agree nor Disagree / Disagree / Strongly Disagree

5. The descendants of the soldiers, since they are specifically identified by family, should have a stronger role in determining scientific investigation of the site than the Hakawi.

Strongly Agree / Agree / Neither Agree nor Disagree / Disagree / Strongly Disagree

Table 5.3 Raw Counts of Responses to Scenario I

Scenario Question Number	Strongly Agree	Agree	Neither Agree Nor Disagree	Disagree	Strongly Disagree	Mising Values
11	12	55	50	55	19	—
13	8	64	51	55	11	2
14	4	28	24	96	37	2

not statistically significant, then one could assume that landownership does not influence archaeologists' decisions.

But the responses to question 4 vary significantly when compared to those from question 3. When landownership is changed from private to Hakawi tribal ownership, archaeologists disagreed more with the idea of excavation. The Friedman's X^2 value of 84.05 (df = 1) is significant with a p-value of 0.00, indicating that the null hypothesis of no difference cannot be accepted (i.e., there is a difference between the responses).

Given the situation described in the first instance, it seems that archaeologists' decisions to excavate the site were indeed influenced by the entity that owned the land upon which the site was found.

Scenario II presented an additional test of archaeologists' responses (fig. 5.2). The primary difference between scenarios I and II is the addition of an ethnographic description of a shaman's story concerning the burial of the dead. One can again check the influence of landownership on excavations by comparing the responses to questions 3 and 4 of this scenario (changing the landownership when the soldiers' descendants want excavation) (table 5.4).

Again, the responses were significantly different (Friedman's X^2 = 71.43 with df = 1 and a p-value of 0.00) to allow the rejection of the null hypothesis of no change in the distribution of the responses.

While this analysis does not *demonstrate* that archaeologists base their decisions entirely on the wishes of those who own the land upon which the site is situated, the responses did change in a statistically significant manner to *suggest* that the change in landownership status had a significant impact on the decision to excavate. Additionally, the research tested whether landownership affected the amount of influence that cultural groups who do not own the land have regarding archaeologists' excavation decisions.

Comparing the responses to questions 1 and 3 in scenario I measures the changes in attitudes regarding excavation when a cultural group with "standing" is in favor of excavation while the Hakawi are opposed to it. The changes are statistically significant (Friedman's X^2 = 5.59 with df = 1 and a p-value of 0.02). But when the land comes under tribal control, it appears that archaeologists fail to weigh the wishes of the soldiers' descendants as heavily as

Table 5.4 Raw Counts of Responses to Scenario I

Scenario Question Number	Strongly Agree	Agree	Neither Agree Nor Disagree	Disagree	Strongly Disagree	Mising Values
II1	8	52	48	65	16	2
II3	6	65	45	62	11	2
II4	5	29	25	97	32	3

Figure 5.2   Scenario II Used in the Research

Scenario II The Ethnographic Record

The background is the same as in scenario I; however, upon reexamination of Hakawi ethnography, given the location of the battle site, you come across a discussion recorded by Frans Boas given to him by the shaman. He described the battle as so repugnant that all the dead were removed of their worldly goods to prevent them from wreaking havoc in the afterworld. Therefore, the identity of the human remains in each of the graves can only be determined by scientific study of the bones themselves.

The Hakawi are against the disturbance of their warriors. The army is delighted to have found its lost men, and wishes to have them returned for ceremonial reburial in the National Cemetery in Arlington. One is also destined for the Tomb of the Unknown Soldier, with associated fanfare.

1. Excavations should be undertaken.

Strongly Agree/Agree/Neither Agree nor Disagree/Disagree/Strongly Disagree

2. The names of the dead soldiers are known, and their descendants do not wish the remains disturbed. Excavations should be undertaken.

Strongly Agree/Agree/Neither Agree nor Disagree/Disagree/Strongly Disagree

3. The descendants of the soldiers (as a group) want the remains shipped to Arlington. Excavations should be undertaken.

Strongly Agree/Agree/Neither Agree nor Disagree/Disagree/Strongly Disagree

4. The remains are on Hakawi land, under the same circumstances. Excavations should be undertaken.

Strongly Agree/Agree/Neither Agree nor Disagree/Disagree/Strongly Disagree

5. The Hakawi want excavation of the remains for a new tribal museum, but the army and the soldiers' descendants do not. Excavations should be undertaken.

Strongly Agree/Agree/Neither Agree nor Disagree/Disagree/Strongly Disagree

6. To what extent should the ownership of the lands in which the burials are located figure into your decision on excavations?

Strongly / Moderately / Some / Little / None At All

---

when the land was in private ownership. More archaeologists were opposed to excavating a site on tribal land than were in favor of excavating it when the site was on private land and excavations were supported by the descendants.

A similar result occurs when comparing questions 1 and 3 of scenario II. In this instance, the differences are statistically significant with a *p*-value of 0.00, Friedman's X^2 = 10.52 with df = 1. In both instances, the archaeologists were influenced by the support of the descendants of the soldiers for excavation, but the support for excavations from the descendants was more than counterbalanced by wishes of the landowner.

The previous data show that there is a statistically significant relationship between landownership and the responses of the archaeologists. Specifically, question 6 of scenario II asks the responder the extent that ownership of the lands in which the burials are located should figure into the decision to excavations. By comparing the responses to this question to the categories of the population data, one can get an understanding of whether or not the respondents' age, level of education, and type of employment position affected the way that they responded.

AGE GROUPS

Since some response cells in the comparison between scenario II6 and the age groups of the respondents had low values, the responses and age categories were compressed. When compared to the various age groups, the distribution of responses to question II6 had a chi-square value of 15.51 (df = 9) and a p-value of 0.081.

B. S. Everitt demonstrated the utility of examining deviations of the observed from the expected values (the residuals) for each cell as an aid in identifying which cells of a contingency table may be responsible for an overall significant chi-square value (1992: 46–48). Since the method of performing the procedure is thoroughly discussed in Everitt, the statistical formulae used to obtain the results will not be detailed here, but only the results will be presented.

The standardized and adjusted residuals were calculated for each cell. When the variables forming the contingency table are independent, these residuals are approximately normally distributed with mean = zero and standard deviation = 1 (Everitt 1992: 47).

An examination of table 5.5 shows the results of the computation of the adjusted residuals and reveals the locations of the cells that contribute most to the significance of the results. In this instance, the cells are composed of the responses from individuals under thirty years of age who felt landownership should play a "moderate" role in excavation decisions (p-value > 0.95), and those individuals more than fifty-one years old who felt that the role of land-

Table 5.5 Table of Values of Standardized and Adjusted Residuals for Comparison of Variable II6 to Age Groups after Compression

```
II6                AGE GROUPS
FREQUENCY |
EXPECTED  |
STND RES  |   RESPONSE CATEGORIES
ADJ RES   |
  * = .95 |   1 & 2|        3|        4|   5 & 6|
TOTAL
----------------------------------------------------------
               1|       3|      18|      28|       2|   52
R               |     5.3|    18.2|    24.0|     4.5|
E STRONGLY|-0.99906|-0.04688| 0.81650|-0.70711|
S               |-1.24220|-0.06848| 1.31195|-0.87141|
P               |        |        |        |        |
O         ------------------------------------------------
N              2|       9|      14|      20|       2|   45
S   MOD-        |     4.6|    15.7|    20.8|     3.9|
E   ERA-        | 2.05151|-0.42904|-0.17541|-0.96210|
    TELY        | 2.48668|-0.61096|-0.27477|-1.15585|
C               |   *    |        |        |        |
A         ------------------------------------------------
T              3|       1|      16|      16|       2|   35
E               |     3.6|    12.2|    16.2|     3.0|
G   SOME        |-1.37032| 1.08794|-0.04969|-0.57735|
O               |-1.60505| 1.49704|-0.07521|-0.67025|
R               |        |        |        |        |
I         ------------------------------------------------
E  LITTLE4|       3|      17|      22|       9|   54
S    OR         |     5.5|    18.9|    25.0|     4.6|
    NONE        | 0.21320|-0.43704|    -0.6| 2.05151|
    AT          | 0.26709|-0.64321|-0.97136| 2.54727|
    ALL         |        |        |        |   *    |
          ------------------------------------------------
   TOTAL          19       65       86       16     186
```

CHI-SQUARE = 15.51 with df = 9 p-value = 0.081

ownership should figure "little or none at all" in excavation decisions (*p*-value > .95).

The data seem to indicate that the "older" archaeologists (over fifty years old) tend to feel that landownership should *not* play as strong a role in excavation decisions as those under the age of fifty, while those between thirty and fifty tend to be more evenly distributed in their responses. The "younger" archaeologists (those under the age of thirty) appear to be more concerned with the role of landownership, perhaps because of the role landownership plays in determining permits, in cultural resource management laws, or in determining the "rights of ownership" of cultural resources recovered during excavations.

EDUCATION LEVEL

The comparison of the landownership question when compared to education level was not significant until the initial seven response categories were compressed into three categories by combining those with a bachelor's degree or less ("1"), those with at least a master's degree ("2"), and those with a doctorate ("3"). Additionally, the landownership variable was compressed into four categories by combining the "little" and "none at all" response categories.

Once again, the standardized and adjusted residuals were calculated to see which cells contributed the most to the statistical significance. Examination of table 5.6 shows that more individuals who had not yet received a master's degree (a bachelor's degree or less) felt that landownership should figure "strongly" in excavation decisions than would be expected to occur if the responses were unrelated, while there were fewer individuals in the same education category who felt that landownership should only figure "some" into the decisions than expected. Additionally, there were fewer with a master's degree who felt landownership should figure "strongly" in excavation than expected (*p*-value = .95).

This is consistent with the previous analysis, as expected, since the degree of education is related to chronological age to some extent. It appears that the younger archaeologists are more likely to be concerned with the status of landownership than the other archaeologists, and that the higher the degree of education, the more

Table 5.6 Table of Values of Standardized and Adjusted Residuals for Comparison of Variable II6 to Education Level after Compression

```
II6                EDUCATION LEVEL
FREQUENCY |
 EXPECTED |
 STND RES |        RESPONSE CATEGORIES
 ADJ RES  |
  *  = .95 |
  ** = .99 |         1|        2|        3|     TOTAL
--------------------------------------------------
           1|       22|       15|       15|       52
R           |      14.3|     21.5|     16.2|
E STRONGLY|   2.03621|-1.40183|-0.29814|
S           |   2.81589|-2.15746|-0.42342|
P           |     **   |    *    |         |
O   --------------------------------------------------
N          2|       13|       22|       10|       45
S    MOD-   |      12.3|     18.6|     14.0|
E    ERA-   |   0.19959| 0.78836|-1.06905|
     TELY   |   0.26908| 1.18281|-1.48012|
C           |         |         |         |
A   --------------------------------------------------
T          3|        4|       19|       12|       35
E           |       9.6|     14.5|     10.9|
G    SOME   |  -1.80739| 1.18176| 0.33318|
O           |  -2.35456| 1.71333| 0.44576|
R           |     *    |         |         |
I   --------------------------------------------------
E   LITTLE4|       12|       21|       21|       54
S     OR   |      14.8|     22.4|     16.8|
     NONE   |  -0.72783|-0.29580| 1.02470|
     AT     |  -1.01412|-0.45868| 1.46628|
     ALL    |         |         |         |
    --------------------------------------------------
TOTAL            51       77       58       186
```

CHI-SQUARE = 14.50 with df = 6 p-value = 0.026

likely the individual feels that the cultural resources of the United States belong to everyone, and that landownership should *not* play a role in excavation decisions.

JOB CATEGORY

The chi-square value of the comparison between the job category question and the landownership question was not significant in its original eight by five comparison, providing a chi-square value of 28.22 (df = 28) and a *p*-value of 0.456. When the response categories for the type of job the responder holds were compressed to three categories by deleting the poorly defined "other" category and combining the remainders into categories defined as "state and/or federal," "college and/or university," and "contract" (regardless of sponsorship), the chi-square value dropped to 5.46 with df = 8 and a *p*-value of 0.707. When the "little" and "none at all" categories were combined, the chi-square value became 1.65 with df = 6 and a *p*-value of 0.949.

This would seem to indicate that the type of job that a responder holds does not affect the viewpoint relating to the role of landownership in excavation decisions. This is mildly surprising, since it was thought that those involved with the contract branch of archaeology would feel that landownership would be an important variable because it figures prominently in decisions relating to project funding when governmental funds are involved.

YEARS IN THE DISCIPLINE (INCLUDING SCHOOL)

When the original six response groups for the number of years in the discipline (including school) were compared with the landownership question, the result was a chi-square value of 39.92 (df = 20) with a *p*-value of 0.006. It was feared that the significance might be a result of the fact that thirteen of the thirty cells had five or fewer responses. Because of this, the six response categories were compressed into three categories—ten years or fewer ("1"); eleven and twenty years ("2"); and more than twenty-one ("3"). At the same time, the response groups for the landownership question were compressed into the four categories used in the other analyses.

An analysis of the standardized and adjusted residuals indicates that those who have been in the discipline from eleven to twenty years were significant in the "some" (more than expected) and "little or none at all" (less than expected) categories, suggesting that landownership appears to lessen in importance with experience (table 5.7). Additionally, more individuals responded that landownership should figure "little or not at all" in excavation decisions in the more than twenty-one category, adding more support to the interpretation.

CULTURAL BIASES

In the past, few agencies allowed individuals or groups to have input regarding the excavation or study of human remains (e.g., the Department of Interior's Policy for the Disposition of Human Remains). Generally, only those individuals or tribal groups who could *demonstrate* a familial or cultural relationship to the human remains were allowed input concerning the ultimate disposition of those remains. Based on the prevalence of this type of policy in the past, it could be hypothesized that archaeologists would be more likely to follow the wishes of individuals who could clearly demonstrate a relationship to human remains (the descendants of the soldiers, in this instance) when the ultimate disposition of the remains are in conflict with another group with a less specific relationship (the Hakawi, in this instance).

However, as shown in the comparisons between questions 1 and 3 for scenarios I and II, that is not necessarily the case. When the soldiers' descendants (as a group) were publicly in favor of excavation, the changes in response distributions were statistically significant. But when the Hakawi own the land, the support for excavations clearly decreases. Since archaeologists' responses to the question do not appear to have been dependent upon support of the excavations by the descendants, it would appear that there is *not* an apparent cultural bias displayed by archaeologists in their responses.

An additional test of this is obtained by question 5 of scenario I, which specifically asks whether the descendants of the soldiers, since they are specifically identified by family, should have a stron-

Table 5.7 Table of Values of Standardized and Adjusted Residuals for Comparison of Variable II6 to Years in the Discipline after Compression

```
II6                 YEARS IN THE DISCIPLINE
FREQUENCY |
  EXPECTED |
  STND RES |      RESPONSE CATEGORIES
  ADJ RES  |
    * = .95 |
   ** = .99 |          1|         2|         3|    TOTAL
------------------------------------------------------
            1|        17|        20|        15|     52
R           |       13.2|      18.8|      20.0|
E STRONGLY|    1.04592|   0.27676|  -1.11803|
S           |    1.42825|   0.40868|  -1.67977|
P           |           |          |          |
O      -----------------------------------------------
N           2|        14|        14|        17|     45
S    MOD-   |       11.4|      16.3|      17.3|
E    ERA-   |    0.77005|  -0.56968|  -0.07213|
     TELY   |    1.02492|  -0.81997|  -0.10562|
C           |           |          |          |
A      -----------------------------------------------
T           3|         5|        21|         8|     34
E           |        8.6|      12.3|      13.0|
G    SOME   |   -1.22759|   2.48066|  -1.38675|
O           |   -1.57325|   3.43803|  -1.95537|
R           |           |       **  |          |
I      -----------------------------------------------
E   LITTLE4|        11|        12|        31|     54
S     OR    |       13.7|      19.6|      20.7|
    NONE   |   -0.72946|  -1.71667|   2.26387|
    AT     |   -1.10430|  -2.55435|   3.42718|
    ALL    |           |       *   |       **  |
------------------------------------------------------
   TOTAL            47        67        71       185

CHI-SQUARE = 21.46 with df = 6 p-value = 0.002
```

ger role than the Hakawi in determining the scientific investigation of the site.

The responses appear to support the interpretation that there is no apparent cultural bias when the responding archaeologists were forced to consider the wishes of either the American Indian group or the soldiers' descendants. Only 2 (1 percent) answered "strongly agree," 16 (8 percent) answered "agree," 101 (53 percent) responded "disagree," and 39 (20 percent) "strongly disagree." Thirty-three (18 percent) answered "neither agree nor disagree."

IMPLICATIONS

The results of the statistical procedures utilized serve to show that the attitude changes from one question to another were significant, but they neither indicate what the responses to the questions mean nor what the changes in attitudes imply.

Most obvious is the apparent indication that the ownership of the land on which a cultural site is located has a greater influence in determining archaeologists' involvement in a project that impacts human remains than do the wishes of the descendants of the groups involved.

Section I.I(c) of the RPA Code of Ethics counsels archaeologists to "Be sensitive to, and respect the legitimate concerns of the *groups* whose culture histories are the subjects of archaeological investigation" (emphasis added), not to the *owner of the land that contains* those culture histories.

The orientation displayed by most of the archaeologists who responded to the questionnaires was tempered more by the actual physical location of where we conduct our study than by the wishes of the people we study. Would a similar study in Canada, England, or any country with laws that claim cultural patrimony for all cultural property reveal a similar orientation?

On the positive side, however, archaeologists tended *not* to exhibit a cultural bias when the wishes of one ethnic group (the soldiers' descendants) were in direct opposition to the wishes of the other ethnic group. The lessened support for excavation when American Indians owned the land and did not want excavation but the soldiers' descendants still wanted excavation reveals this fact.

The influence of the ethnographic record was also shown by the study. When the land was in private ownership, but the Hakawi were shown to have an ethnographic link to the cultural area, archaeologists were less likely to support excavations. Ultimately, however, it appears that landownership carried the most weight in influencing the archaeologists' decisions about whether or not to conduct archaeological excavations on the tract.

SUMMARY

The previous discussion shows the utility for this type of research. Questionnaires force archaeologists to examine their standards rather than blindly accepting current dogma. They also allow them to test existing attitudes prior to setting up any policies that might place constraints on the discipline.

These scenarios are not "real-life" situations, but only fictional constructs to test general attitudes. I am sure that most of us would react differently to actual sit-ins than we say we would, but, if we are forced to examine the situation before it happens, we might be ready if a real one occurs. All the same, the scenarios used in the analyses force us to examine the codes of ethics under which we work, and enable us to work through our concerns before the situations we encounter develop into full-blown conflicts.

Part II

ᢙᤫᤫᤩᤫᢙᤩ

Cases

I have spent the previous four chapters outlining the way that archaeology has portrayed American Indians and their cultures as well as the codes of ethics and legislation that govern the way archaeology deals with and has dealt with American Indian issues. In the following chapters, I will discuss the various ways that American Indian tribal groups have chosen to adapt the American model of historic preservation in their attempts to influence archaeology within their boundaries.

The situations chosen represent three distinct localities. Chapter 6 presents a case study of the Navajo model of historic preservation, one that is among the oldest of tribal programs in the United States. Although very much a bare-bones presentation, it is included primarily because the Navajo were quick to jump at the opportunity to exert control over their cultural heritage and because they have done such a good job of doing it.

Chapter 7 presents the experiences of the Pawnee in their quest to close down the Salina Burial Pit in Kansas as well as a more generalized discussion of the Pawnee Tribe's involvement with archaeology.

Chapter 8 looks at the situation at the East Wenatchee Clovis Cache in the state of Washington, where local archaeologists with an excellent working relationship with the Colville and other local groups united to form an alliance against an archaeologist viewed to be an outsider.

Chapter 9 examines the explosive situation at Kennewick, primarily discussed as a contrast to the relationships developed by local archaeologists in the East Wenatchee Clovis case. Even though it is far from over, Kennewick has influenced the relationship between American Indians and archaeologists far beyond that of any other situation.

In chapter 10, I present thumbnail sketches of the relations between indigenous populations and archaeologists in Canada, Australia, New Zealand, and Sweden as comparative data in order to discover any common threads that might be present in the fabric of indigenous archaeology.

6

◯╲◯ ▷◁ ◯╲◯

Navajo Cultural Resources Management

In the early 1950s a joke came out of the Southwest (long a swarming ground of anthropologists) that the average Navajo family consisted of a mother, father, three children, and an anthropologist. (Lurie 1988: 554)

Although difficult to quantify at present, it may be assumed that the Navajo Indians of New Mexico and Arizona are among one of the most studied (if not *the* most studied) group of American Indians. For years, anthropologists of all disciplines have migrated to Navajo country in early summer to gain an understanding of the archaeology, ceremonies, family traditions, music, or whatever individual interest spurred them on.

But it was not only the Navajo of the area that was of primary interest to archaeologists; in fact, quite the opposite. Early archaeological interest in this area generally revolved around the magnificent archaeological ruins at Chaco Canyon, Canyon de Chelly, Salmon Ruin, and all the other places where there was an abundant evidence of prehistoric utilization of the area by those currently called "Anasazi."

A long and detailed discussion of the history of archaeological investigations in the American Southwest is neither necessary nor intended for this chapter; suffice it to say that archaeological interest in the areas currently under control of the Navajo Nation has a long and varied background.

Although no specific dates for the arrival of the Navajo in the Southwest are available, most archaeologists consider the Navajo to be relative newcomers to the area they now inhabit. David M. Brugge suggests they left the north on the beginning of their migration southward "perhaps some 1,000 years ago" (1983: 489). Early Spanish accounts of people living west of the northern Pueblos and north of Acoma as early as the 1580s (the Antonio de Espejo expedition of 1582–1583) were probably discussing the Navajo (491), while the attacks that forced the Spanish conquerors of New Mexico to abandon their first capital near the junctions of the Chama River and Río Grande in favor of its current location at Santa Fe was probably the handiwork of the Navajo (Forbes 1980: 113).

Thus, the Navajo do have a cultural tie to the lands on which they now reside, even though a large portion of the cultural resources of the area is not culturally related to them (a situation most American Indian groups face today). And, because of various factors (energy exploration and tourism, among others), the Navajo have managed to thrive and expand their administrative capabilities beyond "make-do" programs to programs that rival those of the dominant culture of the United States, especially in relation to the protection of cultural resources.

THE NAVAJO CULTURAL RESOURCES MANAGEMENT PROGRAM

The development of the Navajo cultural resources management program should be seen as a watershed event in the history of an American Indian archaeology. Archaeology on the Navajo Reservation was established in the 1960s as a resource in the Navajo Land Claims litigation (Benallie 1997: 1). The Navajo Nation Cultural Resource Management Program was established in 1977, and ultimately evolved into two programs devoted to the management and protection of archaeological materials and historic properties. In 1986, the Navajo Nation Archaeology Department (NNAD) and the Navajo Nation Historic Preservation Department (NNHPD) were established to provide "professional anthropological expertise combined with regional archaeological experience and an understanding of Navajo customs" (Klesert and Downer 1990: 116).

THE NAVAJO AND ARCHAEOLOGICAL SITES

Perhaps the first clearly documented instance of Navajo involvement with cultural resources was among the early excavations carried out in Chaco Canyon in 1896 by Richard Wetherill. Brugge (1986: 2, 145, 156) mentions these excavations and comments on the apparent conflict between the actions of those working in the ruins, both internally (disturbing the remains of the dead) and externally with those not involved in the excavations (accusations of witchcraft aimed at the excavators). He notes that "Wetherill made claims to being able to ward off the evil effects of the prehistoric spirits, but it is most probable that the Navajos had more frequent resort to Enemyway as a ceremony to control the supernatural dangers of their work" (1986: 156).

Among the Navajo, contact with spirits, ghosts, or places where ghosts are thought to reside can result in what is called "ghost sickness." Leland C. Wyman outlines the Blessingway and the Enemyway rites as: "Blessingway is concerned with peace, harmony, and good things exclusively, while Enemyway, a rite designed to exorcise the ghosts of aliens, makes much of war, violence and ugliness" (Wyman 1983: 539).

Thus, there are apparently two basic conflicts inherent in Navajo treatment of cultural resources within the Navajo Nation homeland—one cosmological (ghosts and places of ghosts, such as archaeological ruins, houses where people have died, and actual graves and burials), and the other cultural (Navajo locations as opposed to Pueblo or prehistoric Anasazi locations).

H. Barry Holt (1983) provides a brief introduction of Navajo traditional religious beliefs about the remnants of prehistoric cultures within their homeland. One legend attributed the destruction of the Anasazi to the wind because of Anasazi blasphemies against nature, especially the Anasazi's painting of sacred designs on utilitarian pottery and their living in rectangular stone houses (1983: 595). Because of this relationship between the Navajo and the Anasazi, archaeological remains on Navajo land have several levels of meanings.

Many Anasazi ruins serve as gathering places for ritual activities among the Navajo, for plants, minerals, or even arrowheads. Holt's brief discussion of the use of ruins (places accessible to supernaturals) in remaking rites (1983: 596) serves to buttress the ritual connection between the Navajo and the prehistoric inhabitants.

Like Brugge, Holt describes the dangers of doing archaeology as perceived by the Navajo in relation to ghost sickness. Because Navajo beliefs concerning witchcraft are so strong and can be likened with activities normally associated with archaeological investigations at prehistoric ruins (disturbing the remains of the dead, collecting objects associated with death, and so forth), Holt warns that the professional archaeologist and those who work for him or her are often viewed with suspicion by the local Navajo and are, therefore, often vulnerable to charges of witchcraft.

He goes on to recommend that any archaeologist who may become involved in a project in the Navajo homeland should:

1. identify local Navajo communities that might have concerns about proposed excavations;
2. contact local Navajo officials concerning actions that might mitigate the adverse effects of the archaeological investigation;
3. contact local Navajo governmental officials to inform them of the investigations and to solicit information about local community views toward ruins and their examination;
4. attempt to contact Navajo residents in the immediate vicinity of the project area in order to explain the nature of the investigations;
5. assure them of the legitimacy of the archaeological activities and ease fears concerning grave robbing or vandalism of ruins;
6. not disturb any ritual paraphernalia until . . . local practitioners can be contacted about proper disposal or relocation of the items; and
7. consider hiring practitioners as crew members, or making prior arrangements to hire local practitioners to assist on an occa-

sional basis to care for the spiritual needs of the other crew members. (1983: 597–98)

The Navajo Nation itself has had a history of utilizing traditional religious practitioners as a part of the cultural resources management program. David E. Doyel (1982) details the hiring and utilization of traditional medicine men in the identification of sacred sites, shrines, or other localities of importance to the Navajo within the cultural resources on Navajo lands targeted for a tribally funded timber project.

The Branch of Cultural Resources program was not concerned with the protection of the field personnel or the general community from harm caused by the disturbance of spirits, but rather with project impacts on the ceremonial or religious nature of site locations and the determination of their "ethnic significance" to the Navajo. This project utilized field visitations by a Navajo medicine man to representative sites of specific types, with comments obtained regarding the value and significance of each site type and how such sites related to Navajo culture. Thus, the Navajo were able to provide guidance to the archaeologists about the different relationships between sites and their importance or religious significance, quite apart from any archaeological or ethnographic significance.

The medicine man utilized by the Branch of Cultural Resources assessed the significance of the sites on the basis of two primary criteria: either within a religious or sacred framework, or their potential contribution to the ongoing economic cycle (Doyel 1982: 637). Certain types of sites were almost always blessed (habitation, sweat lodges, ceremonial grounds, and grave sites), and according to the medicine man, disturbance of such sites would potentially threaten the welfare of the families involved. Thus, an ethical dilemma is created when such sites are disturbed as a result of programs of economic importance to the tribe.

But, in spite of this dilemma, the Navajo have ways of getting things accomplished while contributing to the discipline at the same time. Jesse L. Nusbaum (quoted in Wendorf, Fox, and Lewis 1956: II-IV) details the manner that the Navajo Nation may have given contract or salvage archaeology its start.

In July 1950, the Federal Power Commission issued a Certificate of Public Convenience and Necessity to the El Paso Natural Gas Company. The certificate authorized the construction and operation of the El Paso San Juan Project—a 451-mile, 24-inch gas transmission line from Barker Dome in northwestern New Mexico via Flagstaff and Kingman to the Colorado River, near Topock, Arizona. The project also included related gathering lines, compressor stations, and distribution laterals extending to bordering New Mexico and Arizona communities.

Nusbaum, as departmental consulting archaeologist of the National Park Service, contacted the Navajo in an attempt to convince them of the need for rescuing any archaeological material that might be affected by the construction, but was told by the general superintendent of the Navajo that he did not wish to ask the company to meet the additional cost out of fear that it might protest. Instead, the general superintendent asked the National Park Service to meet the cost. Nusbaum then asked the general superintendent to submit a copy of Nusbaum's original letter to the company for direct consideration.

El Paso Natural Gas agreed to pay the overall cost of archaeological cooperation on the right-of-way, including any private lands, for the San Juan Project. It directly employed five archaeologists and paid field subsistence per diem at the company rate, and provided jeep station wagons, miscellaneous supplies, and Navajo labor assistance as needed on salvage excavations. Ultimately, the company also agreed to pay for the publication of the results.

The program developed for the pipelines also provided another benefit, when W. J. Keller, New Mexico district engineer, Bureau of Public Roads, proposed and then supported the development of a similar archaeological program in connection with road construction in New Mexico. This, the precedent for highway salvage archaeology, was established in New Mexico on April 15, 1954 (Wendorf, Fox, and Lewis 1956: VII).

Nusbaum's final statement can be described as a summation of what salvage archaeology once sought, and what public archaeology now seeks, a system where "commercial enterprise and archaeology can each achieve cherished objectives through cooperative rescue, without impediment, of the archaeological values that earthmoving construction threatens to destroy" (1956: VII).

THE NAVAJO AND HUMAN REMAINS

Anthony Klesert and Michael J. Andrews discuss the procedures developed by the Navajo Nation for cultural resource managers and developers to follow in the identification, verification, and ultimate disposition of human remains on Navajo Tribal Trust land (1988: 310, 320).

As stated earlier, Navajo fear of ghosts and the dead has caused problems in dealing with mortuary material. Those who are aware of grave locations are often afraid to discuss them out of a fear of grave robbing or witchcraft. In spite of this fear, the Navajo Tribal Council passed a resolution (CO-60-73) presenting basic guidelines for the "removal of bodies" within the Navajo Nation in 1973. This called for the consent of the next of kin, with approval by the Advisory Committee of the Navajo Tribal Council for those bodies whose next of kin cannot be determined or located (1988: 311). In 1980, the Parks Commission of the Navajo Tribal Council drew a line between recent or historical graves and those of archaeological origin by adopting the standards of the Archaeological Resources Protection Act, making anything less than one hundred years old nonarchaeological.

Generally, the policy differentiates between claimed and unclaimed human material. Unclaimed bodies are considered those remains for which no next of kin (relatives no more distant than second degree of blood or affinial relationship) can be located. In circumstances where bodies are unclaimed, the Navajo Executive Administrator provides the consent for the extent of archaeological investigations involved. In the event that the cultural remains are from sites on Navajo lands that have more definite association with modern pueblos or other specific tribes, the Navajo Nation would seek the involvement and consent of the affected tribe.

The Navajo policy, according to Klesert and Andrews, does not choose sides in the reburial issue—it allows consenting parties (next of kin or Tribal Council) to approve of any proposed actions through informed consent. The interested scientific party may make a case for scientific study, or the tribe may even suggest such study. The policy operates "to protect the interests of the Navajo people, and, by extension, the material remains of their cultural heritage" (1988: 318).

THE NAVAJO AND ARTIFACTS

Deborah L. Nichols, Anthony L. Klesert, and Roger Anyon, in a summary section regarding the Navajo relationship to "Ancestral Sites, Shrines, and Graves: Native American Perspectives on the Ethics of Collecting Cultural Properties," state that the Navajo consider "it an affront to Navajo religious beliefs for outsiders to search for pots and disturb the bones of 'ancient enemies' or their own ancestors" (1989: 30).

Even the seemingly harmless collection of paleontological remains of petrified wood infringes upon traditional Navajo belief, since this petrified wood is used by medicine men and other religious practitioners in curing and other sacred observances (1989: 31); what is more harmful, however, is the collecting of Navajo religious paraphernalia placed in or near Anasazi sites (Holt 1983: 596).

The best way to stop this pillaging of Native American culture, Nichols, Klesert, and Anyon believe, is for archaeologists and museums to broaden public awareness and knowledge of Native Americans and to accept the Native American ethic "that respects the power and authority of these remains and eschews the possibility of 'ownership' by anyone" (1989: 37). Attorney Bowen Blair (1979) ultimately states that the best way to protect cultural heritage is to prevent its initial removal from tribal land through scientific excavation or pot hunting.

CONCLUSIONS

The Navajo have had a long relationship with archaeology and archaeologists, since 1896 when Wetherill began excavating at Chaco Canyon (Brugge 1986: 2). Since that early involvement, the tribe, both as an administrative body and as individuals, has come to exert tribal control over cultural resources within the overall management of environmental issues.

The establishment of the Navajo Nation Tribal Museum in 1956 was the beginning of tribal involvement in archaeological and historical research programs. With the establishment of the Cultural Resources Management Program in 1977, the Navajo became one of the most administratively advanced American Indian groups relative to the discovery, description, and documentation of cultural resources on American Indian–controlled lands in the United States. It also initiated one of the earliest efforts to integrate consideration of "sacred places" into the cultural resource management process as mandated by federal law.

To address the problem of adequate separation of cultural resource research and cultural resource management, the Historic Preservation Department of the Navajo Nation was established in 1986 in Window Rock, Arizona, to assume the Navajo Nation's responsibilities for management and preservation of cultural resources. With the passage of the Cultural Resources Protection Act by the Navajo Tribal Council, the scope of preservation efforts on Navajo Trust lands was widened.

Daryl R. Begay provides a more in-depth discussion of current Navajo Preservation Department goals and objectives, but in general, the ultimate repercussions may center around the facts that:

1. The Navajo are implementing the types of regulations and legislation that were previously held by Congress in relation to cultural resources.
2. The Navajo are providing review and compliance for "Section 106" of the National Historic Preservation Act.
3. The Navajo are developing and administering a registry of Navajo Cultural Properties and of Navajo Cultural Landmarks (like the National Register of Historic Places).
4. The Navajo (because of NAGPRA) are able to control the excavation and disposition of human remains within the boundaries of their reservation.
5. The Navajo are no longer bound by a worldview not their own in relation to the control of cultural resources. (1991: 3–4)

The Navajo are adapting the techniques of the dominant Euroamerican society to their specific situation, thereby allowing them to take control over all cultural resources within their lands, to delineate the extent of disturbances to those resources, and, possibly, to determine who will conduct research on those resources, and what that research will entail.

It is interesting to note the interaction among the Navajo Preser-
vation Department, professional archaeologists, and traditional
Navajo individuals. But Rena Martin asks whether the Navajo
Nation Historic Preservation Department preserves "the Navajo
Nation's cultural resources as the traditionalists would?" (1997:
128).

As past manager of the Traditional Culture Program of the
NNHPD, and having worked within both the NNAD and the
NNHPD, Martin is able to discuss the discomfort of traditional
people with the testing and excavation of archaeological or historical properties on Navajo lands. Since most of the programs within
the NNHPD receive federal funds, they are, as Martin notes "mandated to comply with federal regulations that often conflict with
tribal traditions" (1997: 129).

Additionally, Richard M. Begay (1997: 164) questions why the
Navajo Nation requires archaeologists and the NNAD to classify
archaeological sites according to the Pecos Classification when such
has no meaning to Navajo.

Therefore, while the Navajo Nation has taken great strides in integrating the federal system into the protection of cultural resources
within the reservation, it is still a mostly foreign system it has taken.
Traditional Navajo individuals still view archaeologists with suspicion, including Navajo archaeologists employed to ensure compliance. There are still major problems to be solved, but, as Begay
says, "the more native archaeologists there are, the more quickly we
can make positive changes" (1997: 165).

It is important for anthropology, as a discipline, to realize that all
American Indian groups *may* someday reach the point where they
control cultural resources on tribal or federal lands, and their programs may not be the same as those we now see. It is possible that,
provided a more open opportunity to implement the spirit of cultural preservation regulations rather than the letter of such regulations, American Indians might someday develop programs that
would do away with the testing and excavation of threatened
archaeological sites in favor of a program of recordation that preserved the information and spirit of the site while allowing the
corporeal "body" of the site to be destroyed.

The future of archaeological and anthropological research on American Indian or federal property may soon be in the hands of the group that can organize most efficiently or exert the greatest influence on federal legislators. What such a program would look like I can only guess, but I believe the information it collected would be beneficial to our understanding of the past.

7

The Pawnee and the Salina Burial Pit

> The "Indian Burial Pit" was opened for business in 1937, and has proven to be commercially viable since that time. Visitation in 1984 . . . was estimated at more than ten thousand people with a gross income of $20,000 for the site. (Stein 1989: 4)

HISTORICAL AND ARCHAEOLOGICAL BACKGROUND

In the 1930s, amateur archaeologist and Salina, Kansas, police sergeant Guy L. Whiteford uncovered the skeletal remains of 146 persons buried together in a single locality in the vicinity of the town. Rather than removing the skeletons and their associated material for scientific study, however, the skeletons within the Whiteford site (also named the Whiteford-Price site, the Salina Burial Pit, or the "Indian Burial Pit," as it more popularly came to be known), were left in place, with a wooden building erected over the site. Tourists were then allowed to view the remains, and the site became a commercial venture when it was sold to the Price family in 1937.

Materials from the burials led archaeologists to believe that the community cemetery was from a group known archaeologically as the Smoky Hill aspect. The Smoky Hill aspect, as originally defined by Waldo R. Wedel (1959: 563–65), consisted of generally small villages, with no indication of defensive earthworks. House sites were square to rectangular, with rounded corners, four main roof supports set around a central fire basin, and an extended entryway.

The Smoky Hill burial complex was defined primarily from the materials at the Salina Burial Pit. The vast majority of the burials were primary, or flesh burials rather than secondary interments. The individuals were partially or completely flexed, with the knees and lower limbs forming a right or obtuse angle. The body was usually placed on its right side, with the head to the south and its face to the east.

The exact relationship between the Smoky Hill aspect to the other complexes of the Middle Ceramic Period of the Great Plains (about A.D. 1000 to 1500), the Upper Republican and Nebraska aspects, is uncertain. James H. Gunnerson (1987: 75) suggests that a derivation from a local Woodland complex (combined with possible influences from the Southwest) should be considered. He believes that the people who produced the cultural material of the Middle Ceramic Period (referred to as the Smoky Hill aspect, the Upper Republican phase, the Nebraska phase, the Washita River phase, the Panhandle aspect, and the various complexes in eastern Colorado) are closely related, that the definitions do not reflect cultural or linguistic entities that would have been meaningful to the people themselves, and that they were most probably Caddoan speakers ancestral to modern Arikara, Pawnee, and Wichita (78).

Wedel (1959: 564) suggests that the Smoky Hill was parental to the Upper Republican and Nebraska aspects, but also considers that the Smoky Hill might be merely a geographical variant of culture groups within the area at that time period, and that the similarities between the Smoky Hill aspect, Nebraska aspect, and Upper Republican phase might suggest common ancestry.

Given the limited excavation of sites attributable to this aspect, the relationship of the Smoky Hill aspect (and the Salina Burial Pit) population to protohistoric tribal groups is tenuous. The likeliest candidates for cultural affiliation, as suggested by Gunnerson and Wedel, appear to be either the Pawnee (represented by the Late Ceramic Period Lower Loup Focus of Nebraska) or the Wichita (represented by the Late Ceramic Period Great Bend aspect of east-central Kansas).

Wedel feels "there remains little doubt . . . that the Pawnees
. . . were directly descended from the Lower Loup peoples who had
resided in the same locality from two to three centuries earlier"
(1961: 124). He cites the similarities in pottery, house types, and the
material cultural generally as evidence linking the Pawnee with the
Lower Loup Focus, as well as historical accounts of early travelers
in the region. His two other works (1936, 1938) also support this
idea.

As for the relationship between the Smoky Hill and Great Bend
aspects, E. Monger (1970) reported on a site near Larned, Kansas,
at the extreme western edge of the distribution of the Great Bend
aspect, that contained an occupation attributed to Smoky Hill aspect in its lowest levels. Sixty centimeters of nearly sterile fill separated the Smoky Hill occupations from the next level, attributed to
the Pratt focus. The third zone of human occupation was represented by materials from the Great Bend aspect, with forty-five centimeters of deposits separating this from the previous level.

The Great Bend aspect deposits contained evidence of at least
three occupations, each with structures present. Another occupation
level lay above the Great Bend aspect levels, but the material culture was inadequately described to allocate to other specific groups
(Gunnerson 1987: 101).

Numerous authors, including both Wedel (1961: 105–7) and
Gunnerson (1987: 100–1), attribute the Great Bend aspect to the
protohistoric Wichita (based on location of the sites, the cultural
material recovered, and the house patterns within the sites). They
also attribute the Quivera Indian villages described by Francisco
Vásquez de Coronado and Juan de Oñate in 1541 and 1601, respec-
tively, to the historic Wichita.

Therefore, it appears likely that the people who left their dead in
the cemetery that was later to become the Salina Burial Pit were
most likely related to the Caddoan group known as the Wichita,
with the Pawnee perhaps slightly more distantly related.

THE TREATY OF SMOKY HILL

Scientifically, the archaeological uniqueness and potential for research information on a complex of burials from a relatively distinct

population is outstanding. In fact, the National Park Service, recognizing this uniqueness and potential, designated the site as a National Historic Landmark in 1964.

The Kansas State Historical Society also recognized the site's scientific importance, and this, coupled with the inadequate display facility and lack of interpretation at the site, caused the society to propose in 1985 that it be acquired by the state. The site would then have been developed as an interpretative center for the Smoky Hill Culture "to dignify, commemorate, and interpret the lifeways of these people" (Witty 1989a: 124). Funds were appropriated for the acquisition, but eventually deleted by the governor because of landowner unhappiness with the offering price.

Socially, however, the display of the bodies of the 146 dead became the target of Indian opposition by members of the Pawnee Tribe of Oklahoma, the Wichita and Affiliated Tribes, and the Three Affiliated Tribes of the Fort Berthold Reservation, North Dakota. This confederation retained the Native American Rights Fund that engaged in a lobbying effort for the development of state legislation to purchase the site and eventually rebury the remains.

On January 17, 1986, a meeting was held on the Haskell Indian Junior College campus, with representatives of various tribes (the Pawnee, Wichita, and Arikara) voicing their opposition to the display at the burial pit as well as opposition to any future facility that would exhibit those (or any Native American) human skeletal remains. As a result of this meeting, the Kansas State Historical Society abandoned any plans to acquire the site for development.

Following the Haskell meeting, a committee was set up to draft legislation to consider the concerns of Native Americans in archaeological excavations and display of their remains in the state of Kansas. House Bill 2704 was introduced to a legislative subcommittee in the 1987 legislative session.

Under the proposed bill, it would have been illegal to possess human skeletal remains or articles from unmarked grave sites. Additionally, any public display of human remains would require an authorization by a proposed "Unmarked Burial Sites Preservation Board" to be created under the Kansas State Historical Society. The bill stalled because there was no appropriation to compensate the Price family if their "business" was ordered closed (Stolfus

1988). An additional factor that led to the bill's demise was concern voiced by anthropologists from Wichita State University about the disposition of existing collections within certain museums in the state (Witty 1989a: 125).

In February 1989, the Treaty of Smoky Hill was negotiated, in which it was agreed that the landowners would sell the site in an ingress/egress easement to the state for $90,000, commercial operation of the Salina Burial Pit would cease at the date of sale, site improvements would be removed, and the remains would be buried *in situ* at the expense of the state. It was also agreed that $40,000 would be approved by the state to assist in the reburial and that the site would be maintained by the state and county historical societies. This agreement became final in April 1989.

At the same time, the burial pit was the focus of the Kansas House Federal and State Affairs Committee, which was studying a proposal to protect unmarked burials. This proposal resulted in Kansas House Bill (H.B.) 2144, the Kansas Unmarked Burial Sites Preservation Act, signed into law on May 24, 1989 (Witty 1989b: 3).

Kansas H.B. 2144 "prevents indiscriminate or purposeful excavation, collection, or display of human remains recovered from a grave site outside of a marked cemetery. This includes the graves of all persons on any land within the state. It provides for consultation with kin or descent groups about the disposition of remains disinterred for whatever reason" (1989b: 3).

The law also made it a crime to willfully disturb, possess, display, buy, sell, or trade remains or burial goods from an unmarked grave site, excluding materials within collections acquired before January 1, 1990. The law also applied to state and educational institutions.

The law established a nine-member Unmarked Burial Sites Preservation Board, chaired by the state archaeologist, to consist of a physical anthropologist, a historian, two members of the general public, and appointees from four resident Kansas tribes (the Pottawatomie, Iowa, Kickapoo, and Sac and Fox). The board was set up to help decide on the disposition of any remains as well as on any periods of study relating to the skeletal material. Delays in the reinterment (e.g., for scientific study) may be permitted by the board. (For more detailed discussion of various facets of the law, see Witty [1989a: 124–32].)

REBURIAL AND REPATRIATION

"Bones and bodies are not the only issues archeologists face when they begin research late this summer on the Indian Burial Pit" (Zier 1989a), so opens the article about the reburial and repatriation efforts undertaken by state archaeologists and American Indian groups at the Salina Burial Pit.

Because the "Pawnee were afraid of damaging the spirit if the grave goods were placed with the wrong individual" (Witty 1990), it was necessary that the artifacts were placed only with the body that they originally had accompanied. Some artifacts had remained in their original locations in the burials, but "10 to 15" artifacts were either in the collections of the landowners or the historical society in Topeka. Archaeologists used the field notes of the original excavator (Guy L. Whiteford) to place the returned artifacts in their original grave locations.

An April 7 article in the *Wichita Eagle* reported that "archeologists and Indian leaders gathered last week for their burial ceremony. The Indians carried brightly colored blankets and shawls to wrap the skeletons, and ancient Indian medicines to consecrate the ground" (Anonymous 1990a). The blankets were placed on remains identified as males, the shawls on those identified as female. Neither the article nor Witty (1990) noted which was placed on remains not identified as to sex.

Finally, the burials were covered with sand and capped with six inches of reinforced concrete to protect the material from anyone (archaeologists included) who might try to dig it up. The concrete was provided with drain holes to promote natural destruction of the site. Then the entire structure was covered with a mound of earth.

On April 15, 1990, a traditional Pawnee mourning feast was held, a culmination of negotiations between Kansas archaeologists, American Indian groups, the Kansas State Historical Society, and the private landowners. An exhibit documenting the closing of the Salina Burial Pit was on display at the Kansas State Capitol in Topeka during January and February 1991.

THE PAWNEE AND THE NEBRASKA STATE HISTORICAL SOCIETY

The Pawnee have had other interactions with archaeologists concerning the repatriation of human remains and associated cultural materials from the southern Great Plains, but not all of them have been as quietly and calmly handled as at the Salina Burial Pit.

The Pawnee Tribe's request for the repatriation of Pawnee human remains and funerary objects held in the collections of the Nebraska State Historical Society was met with steadfast refusal to negotiate for their return. Even though the historical society's refusal did not prevent the passage of the landmark 1989 Nebraska Unmarked Human Burial Sites and Skeletal Remains Protection Act (the first general statute in the United States to require repatriation and to set standards and procedures for the return of American Indian skeletal remains and funerary objects), the long and acrimonious dispute between the tribe and the historical society was in marked contrast to the amicable relationship shared with the Kansas legislature.

The tribe's involvement with the historical society began in 1988 as an administrative request for the reburial of human remains in the historical society's collections and the repatriation of the associated funerary objects (Peregoy 1992: 337). As with most states, the Nebraska law provided statutory procedures for the disinterment and reinterment of human bodies, but such protection had not been afforded the remains of prehistoric populations.

The previous year, in January 1987, Senator James Pappas introduced Legislative Bill 612 to protect unmarked burial sites from unauthorized disturbances and to establish a procedure for the treatment and disposition of human skeletal remains held by public institutions (1992: 350). According to Robert M. Peregoy, the bill failed to pass because the "NSHS [Nebraska State Historical Society] waged a successful media campaign against L.B. 612 . . . [u]sing unfounded scare tactics" (351).

Throughout 1988, the tribe and the historical society worked on developing legislation to protect unmarked graves in the state. In September 1988, however, the historical society submitted a bill without tribal consultation in its development. Proposed L.B. 691 was seen by the tribal groups as being self-serving and was resoundingly defeated in March 1989 (1992: 354) in favor of L.B. 340, the Unmarked Human Burial Sites and Skeletal Remains Protection Act.

Repatriation concerns continued to be discussed by the Pawnee throughout the legislative lobbying process. The tribe decided to exhaust all administrative remedies before appealing to other forms of the government for relief, and formally commenced repatriation negotiations with the historical society in March 1988. Director of the NSHS, James A. Hanson, is quoted as opposing the return of the material to the Pawnee because "he disparagingly equated human dead bodies with books, and argued 'a bone is like a book . . . and I don't believe in burning books'" (1992: 357).

Peregoy (1992: 357–85) goes on to chronicle the dispute between the Pawnee and the historical society, and weaves into the story the roles of peripheral parties in the event, including scientists from the Smithsonian Institution and the National Park Service. In spite of the U.S. Department of the Interior's waiver of any federal interest in the material in December 1988, the historical society refused to return the items until required by legislation.

The Reburial Act required the repatriation of "reasonably identifiable" disinterred human skeletal remains to tribes or tribal groups within one year after the request for repatriation. The one-year period was to allow the initiation and completion of scientific studies on the remains. The historical society, however, interpreted "reasonably identifiable" to include in its lists of human remains for repatriation to the Pawnee only those associated with the historic Pawnee and Lower Loup cultures (Peregoy 1992: 379).

The Pawnee submitted a grievance to the historical society, portions of which focused on the society's refusal to repatriate human remains from prehistoric Loup River/Itskari phase sites or remains associated with the Central Plains Tradition (Peregoy 1992: 381).

In March 1991, the Nebraska State Public Counsel ruled that the Pawnee had established through a preponderance of the evidence that the human remains and burial goods from the prehistoric Itskari phase sites were reasonably identifiable as ancestors to the Pawnee (Peregoy 1992: 384).

In September 1990, the Pawnee Tribe were able to rebury 401 individuals listed as Pawnee repatriated from the historical society, and, in September 1991, "over three hundred Pawnee Indians and their burial goods from the Loup River/Itskari phase of Nebraska development" were interred in a mass grave (Peregoy 1992: 384–85).

CONCLUSIONS

The situation involving the American Indian groups, the archaeologists of Kansas, and the Kansas State Historical Society is noteworthy for its lack of conflict. Even though the original wish of the state of Kansas was to preserve the Salina Burial Pit for its "educational and scientific" value, the state did not react negatively to the request of the American Indians and the Native American Rights Fund for closure of the pit.

Similarly, the American Indian groups did not play out the conflict in the media, rather they discussed the matter and their concerns with all parties involved, then negotiated a final settlement beneficial to most of the parties involved.

The closing of the Salina Burial Pit indicated that American Indian concerns need not be shouted or fought through the press in order to be heeded. The Pawnee and other tribes were able to work with members of the Kansas State Historical Society in order to get the remains reburied, and members of the historical society were able to get the remains studied.

As an outgrowth of the publicity, archaeologists in Kansas were able to get new legislation passed that acts to protect human remains from looting and willful destruction. Both sets of parties benefited from the actions, although some scientists may feel that the legislation may place undue restrictions (such as time constraints, consultation processes, or determinations of tribal or ethnic descent) on scientific study of human remains.

The situation in Nebraska was markedly different, however. Peregoy's discussion of the dispute between the Pawnee and the Nebraska State Historical Society presented the issue in a manner that pictured the state agency as doing its utmost to prevent repatriation and reburial of grave goods through a process that was "characterized by bad faith, deception, and unlawful conduct" (1992: 353).

The Kansas legislators and archaeologists were acting under different circumstances, however. They were working to close a commercial business that reflected bad taste from a bygone era and were not negotiating for the return of human remains and burial goods from museum collections. Perhaps also, they chose to negotiate rather than risk the type of war that had happened in Nebraska.

It is uncertain to what extent the Pawnee Tribe will develop any type of cultural resources management program as a result of this action. Their continued involvement with reburial concerns (such as their requests for repatriation of Central Plains Tradition

Steed-Kisker phase materials from the Smithsonian) shows a tribal commitment to reburying human remains, but the direction of that interest is not known. At present, it is only known that the tribe is lobbying for legislation to have all materials related to the Pawnee returned for reburial and/or repatriation.

An analysis of the situation makes some things clear. It is possible for American Indian groups and archaeologists to work together when united for a common cause, and American Indians are not adverse to working within an established system to get things accomplished. Archaeologists were able to use the positive publicity generated by the closing of the Salina Burial Pit to influence the Kansas legislature to obtain passage of a law that protects unmarked burials from destruction, and at the same time American Indians got a law that protects unmarked burials from commercial exploitation.

But the process begun with the closure of the Salina Burial Pit was not the total success American Indians and archaeologists of Kansas had hoped.

American Indian groups such as the Kaw, the Wichita, and the Pawnee, which had moved from Kansas to Oklahoma, were not represented on the Unmarked Burial Sites Preservation Board and were forced to rely on the four resident Kansas tribes for help in the eventuality of a conflict.

The Unmarked Burial Sites Preservation Board continued to meet throughout the early 1990s. But the retirement of the state archaeologist (the board's chairman) and the illness and death of the replacement state archaeologist coupled with the move of the Kansas State archaeologist's office into a new building has resulted in an inactivity of the board. Its last meeting was held in 1994 (Thies 1999).

Following the anticipated hiring of a new state archaeologist in 2000, the Kansas State archaeologist's office hopes to reactivate the Unmarked Burial Sites Preservation Board into a "vital force in dealing with Kansas burial sites" (Thies 1999). Perhaps American Indian populations can utilize this force, in conjunction with NAGPRA, to protect human remains in the state.

The Pawnee Tribe has been involved with additional repatriations since the closure of the Salina Burial Pit, but this first concerted effort set the stage for those to follow. Not all of the relationships between the tribe and archaeologists have been as amiable, but the tribe has learned to effectively work within the systems established by repatriation legislation.

8

౦‿౦ ⋈ ౦‿౦

The Conflict at the
East Wenatchee Clovis Site

In 1987, an irrigation project in an apple orchard owned by Mack Richey in central Washington revealed a cache of Clovis points of a size previously unrecorded. The discovery of the points, the initial testing of the site, and the subsequent events that followed form the basis of this chapter, which examines the conflicts between groups within the Pacific Northwest.

These groups—archaeologists and American Indians of the area—were all acting in what was perceived as the best manner to treat the archaeological resource, but it seems that the conflict came about as a result of distrust, miscommunication, and conflicting ethical/value systems.

ARCHAEOLOGICAL OVERVIEW

After Moises Aguirre's discovery of the Clovis points, Robert R. Mierendorf, an archaeologist for the National Park Service, and Russell Congdon, an amateur archaeologist, performed test excavations at the site to determine the context of the stone tools. These tests, on August 16, 1987, confirmed the existence of *in situ* cultural deposits of Clovis age. Because of the information revealed by the testing of the site, the orchard owner placed more than thirty tons of concrete blocks over the site to protect the materials.

117

The East Wenatchee Clovis site is located on a terrace 180 meters above the Columbia River in Douglas County, Washington. R. B. Waitt and B. F. Atwater have called this terrace "the world's most colossal point bar" (1989: 47). Its deposits hold large boulders and giant current ripples (one hundred meters between crests) capped by loess. Five hundred meters north of the site is a moat of non-deposition or erosion that separates the great flood bar from higher flood and landslide deposits on the valley's edge.

Because of the relative uniformity of deposits, ground-penetrating radar was used to discover the presence of stone within the deposits. Two locales produced anomalies investigated by one-by-one meter pits; natural concentrations of cobbles explained the anomalies and confirmed the benefits of the radar survey (Mehringer 1989: 7). Another radar reading led to excavation of a unit that contained a high number of rodent burrows at the expected artifact level. The radar had picked up these burrows because the moist soil filling the burrows stood out against the matrix of dryer, coarser sand (1989: 8).

In the apple orchard, the radar revealed several distinct indications of buried dense objects, which later turned out to be Clovis points and bifaces. The radar also revealed several distinct indications of buried dense objects near the Clovis artifacts that were not disturbed.

On April 8, 1988, the slabs were removed and testing was resumed with professionals, Paleo-Indian specialists from across the United States, and representatives of the Colville Confederated Tribes. These tests, under the direction of Peter Mehringer Jr. of Washington State University (WSU), were aimed at obtaining information to be used to plan future major excavations.

The site grid was oriented so that test units were placed parallel to the irrigation line. The limits of the disturbance defined the approximate eastern boundary of Mehringer's Excavation units 7 and 9. Other units excavated in the area of the artifact concentration include units 4, 5, and 10; the eastern twenty centimeters of unit 14 was also excavated in order to partially expose the relationships of artifacts extending into unit 9.

Exposed artifacts were recorded in three dimensions, with the angles of repose (dip and strike) also recorded. Only five artifacts were removed for analysis, with life-sized plastic cutouts placed in their location prior to backfilling of the site. Mehringer did not give a total inventory of artifactual material, nor did he list the number and type of artifacts encountered during these test excavations. The testing was completed on April 15, when the area was backfilled and covered with the slabs again.

Some artifacts uncovered by the orchard workers had contained a rough coating on all or part of one surface or edge, while others did not. The five artifacts removed from the site for study in 1988 had silica cement only on their lower edges and surfaces, and only where they had been in contact with the sediments (Mehringer 1989: 43). Soil samples of the sediments immediately below the artifacts revealed an abundance of fine sand and silt-sized Glacier Peak pumice.

The several eruptions of Glacier Peak at around 11,250 years ago (Mehringer et al. 1984) all produced tephras too similar to distinguish from one another; they all probably occurred within a few decades of each other, however, and certainly less than the 100 or more years to be expected for the standard deviation alone on an 11,000 years ago radiocarbon date (Mehringer 1989: 52).

Mehringer and F. F. Foit (1990: 499) infer that only the artifacts resting on volcanic glass developed crusts, whereas those that were not in direct contact with the pumice did not form siliceous crusts. They also believed that the artifacts protected the pumice from mixing and set up a shadow beneath them in which moisture persisted longer than in the surrounding sediments.

Mehringer closed down the excavations after only three days because the materials they were encountering were "too remarkable to disturb without additional time and planning. Selection of colorful chert, the number, density and size of the artifacts, and the presence of red ochre left no doubt" that the site was "special" (1989: 54). The testing produced "several bifaces, the most complete Clovis fluted points recovered from a single site, and the largest Clovis point yet known—all from two one-meter squares. Work was finally halted altogether when apparent bone fragments and associated artifacts—suggesting a burial—appeared in the floor of Excavation Unit 9" (54).

Additional field studies were undertaken to place the site within geological, chronological, and cultural contexts. Backhoe trenches placed between the site and the terrace moat to the north exposed a complete last glacial-to-present depositional sequence, beginning with gravel of the last floods that formed the point bar on which the site rests, and ending with loess mixed in the plow zone. The chronological time period for use of the site was dated through the Glacier Peak pumices to about 11,250 years ago.

Analysis of some of the stone points also revealed information: stains on the largest point showed it was hafted, and initial tests by Margaret Newman at the University of Calgary in Alberta indicated bovine blood residue on three of the stone artifacts, including one of the large chalcedony points (Mehringer 1988: 502–3).

After completion of this portion of research on the site, the relationship between the landowner and personnel from WSU apparently began to change.

In March 1990, the Buffalo Museum of Science, with Richard M. Gramly as the principal investigator, applied for a permit to conduct archaeological excavations at the East Wenatchee Clovis site. On May 14, 1990, the permit was issued allowing for the excavation of thirty-five square meters in the time period between October 15 and December 7, 1990.

The acquisition of a permit to conduct archaeological excavations on private land was required by the passage of Washington State Senate Substitute Bill 5807 (an "act relating to archeological objects and sites; the protection of Indian and Historic graves") on July 23, 1989. Amendments to the bill passed on August 8, 1989, adding definitions and coverage of the law. Application requirements, information needed in the application, conditions relating to the notification of affected native American Indian tribes, and other conditions relating to the issuance, denial, and revocation of the permit were also within these amendments. It also calls for the office of the Washington State Historic Preservation Office to notify affected *native* Indian tribes of applications for permits to excavate sites the tribe may consider to have historic or cultural significance. According to the law, as amended, stipulations pertaining to the disposition of human remains may be incorporated into any permit.

Although Gramly received a permit to conduct excavations at the site, things did not go smoothly. The proposed excavations were the subject of protest from local American Indians (the Colville Confederated Tribe and the Yakama Tribe) as well as points of concern to archaeologists within the state of Washington.

Ultimately, the excavations were carried out with Gramly leading a group of volunteers from Earthwatch in the excavation of the site. Instead of excavating thirty-five square meters, an agreement reached with the Colville allowed the excavation of only ten square meters, with only the completion of squares or partial squares opened up by Mehringer in the artifact concentration area amounting to one meter, and the excavation of an L-shaped geologic trench along the north and east edges of the artifact concentration area (seven meters east-west and five meters north-south).

The exact number of artifacts recovered has not been published, and counts presented in the newspaper articles from the area differ—"The site also yielded 30 stone pieces including 14 finished spear points" (Wheat 1990e: 2); "the 22 artifacts will soon be taken" (Wheat 1990f: 2); "[t]he site produced more than 75 artifacts" (Associated Press 1990b: B1); "17 objects, most spear and knife points" (Anonymous 1990b: A6).

D. C. Waldorf presents a very brief analysis of certain bifaces from the site, and gives this brief listing: "As it now stands, the cache comprises some 62 objects, 14 are fluted points, 9 are animal bone spear points or tools, the rest are quarry blanks, bifaces in various stages, 2 gravers, and several blade tools" (Waldorf 1991b: 4).

The conflict between Gramly and the descendants of the Wenatchee Indians must be examined more closely. It does not appear to be solely a conflict based in the American Indian versus archaeologist ethical conflict, because there was no prior conflict evident between the Colville and the Washington State excavators at the site.

The Colville became involved because the land upon which the East Wenatchee Clovis site is located is within the homeland of the Wenatchee Tribe as recorded upon first contact with Euroamericans. During the Reservation period, the Wenatchee were formally placed on the reservation of the Colville Confederated Tribes; some, however, moved to the Yakama Tribal Reservation (Ruby and Brown 1986: 266–67). Tribal representatives were contacted prior to the April 1988 testing, and were present during the excavations.

Because Mehringer was expecting to conduct further excavations at the site, an agreement was reached between WSU and the Colville Confederated Tribes. Because it appeared likely that during further excavation human remains could be uncovered, the agreement served as an understanding of protocols to be observed during excavations including monitoring of work by representatives of the tribe, consultation in the event human remains were encountered, and the establishment of specific lines of contact between both groups.

COLVILLE CULTURAL RESOURCE MANAGEMENT

The Colville Confederated Tribes were not uninformed about the science of archaeology and archaeologists. The Colville Confederated Tribes History/Archaeology Department (which oversees archaeological investigations on tribal lands) was created in 1978, the same year the tribe adopted its Archaeological Resources Protection Ordinance. Prior to this, the tribe had only a history department with no authority to manage cultural resources on its land.

Adeline Fredin (1990) discusses the tribe's first involvement with cultural resource management, beginning with the recovery of human skeletal remains excavated from the reservation nearly forty years prior to the establishment of the history department. In discussing the first reburial situation, she writes:

> After consultation regarding the analysis process, the prospect of having no scientific analysis carried out to identify who we were taking care of seemed even more objectionable . . . it became obvious that it was our responsibility to return some dignity and respect, by using science to return an identity to these people. . . . By the time they laid these remains to rest, we knew as much about them as science would allow. To me, as a cultural resources manager, I feel this is the least we can do for our ancestors. (293)

The Chief Joseph Dam project (1978–1980) on the Upper Columbia River was the initial large-scale cultural resources project to receive extensive tribal input. The Colville were involved in some of the initial planning stages, and individuals from the tribe were employed in the field as workers and monitors.

The Mount Tolman project (1978–1980) was initiated by the tribe itself. The cultural resources investigations were a part of the compliance processes for a tribal mining operation on Mount Tolman (Aikens 1990: 302). Following this, the tribe became involved as a consulting body in the Wells Reservoir Archaeological project, on the Columbia River just downstream from Chief Joseph Dam. As a result of these projects in which the Colville became involved, a permanent data repository has been established at the Colville Reservation Headquarters in Nespelem, Washington.

According to Fredin, "the Chief Joseph archeological investigation gave us the technical training for scientific research. . . . This training allowed the tribe to have total tribal employment on the Mount Tolman archeological survey and analysis" (1990: 295, 296). When speaking of tribal involvement in cultural resources management, she says:

> Each tribe must examine their own ancestral past and make their own decision on how involved they wish to become in cultural resources management. The Colville Tribe did not exclude themselves from the whole investigative process, they took particular interest in specific areas. We remain interested and observant in all archaeological investigations, and we also review and comment where we think it is necessary. (298)

Thus, the tribe was commenting on an archaeological project of direct interest to the tribe, and was not reacting to the proposed investigations as an uninformed bystander.

Gramly, however, failed to specifically acknowledge that he would take the wishes of the Colville into consideration. This is one of the reasons why the Colville did not support the proposed excavations. Under the permitting process, tribes had a time period to respond to permit applications. However, the Colville did not respond to the original permit application, except to ask for more time. On July 19, the Colville Confederated Tribes passed a resolution to ask the state of Washington to keep the protective cement over the site until the concerns of the tribe had been met.

The Colville were acting out of concern over two items—that the site appeared to have been "special" or sacred, and that there was the possibility that human remains might be encountered. They felt that Mehringer's original speculations about the nature of the site were justified. The Colville and the Yakama both claimed cultural ties to the area. Colville acting police chief John Dick was quoted as saying that the excavation of any Clovis remains "would be like somebody trying to dig up the bones of my father" and that "no matter who or where they're at, they're still my people . . . nobody should disturb them" (Wren 1990a: 1). He also commented, "I'm afraid if there's a burial there they'll take it clear across the nation to study. I'm not going to see the remains of my ancestors returned back here in my lifetime if they take them back there" (7).

The Yakama agreed with the Colville. Yakama Indian Nation councilman Harry Smiskin said the Yakama feel that "'there's a strong probability' that Clovis man was ancestral to all local bands" (Wren 1990a: 1).

Gramly, however, viewed things differently. He told reporters that he felt the issue was the right to conduct science. "Scientists agree, he said, that it is pointless to try to connect any current people, such as the Colville, to remains more than 4,000 years old. 'I took that as gospel. Obviously it's not gospel to the Colville'" (Anonymous 1990b: 7).

His application for the archaeological permit also details this view. In a note to the section on the proposed analysis on human remains (if found), he writes:

It cannot be assumed, *a priori*, that human skeletal remains from the East Wenatchee Clovis site, if any are found, are American Indian, however defined. East Asia is home to a variety of genetically-distinct populations. Any or all of these groups could have participated in the peopling of the Americas. Some of these initial immigrants may have left no descendants who survived in the present era. (Gramly 1990: 9–10)

Other archaeologists agree—to an extent. David J. Meltzer writes about the "possibility that the earliest migration was not a single episode, but a multiple series, and that some of those in the multiple series may have failed" (1989: 482). He goes on to say that "we lose sight of the fact that Clovis may represent a composite of migratory 'dribbles'" and that "by virtue of the success of the Clovis groups, we miss the possibility that others . . . (pre-Clovis groups) simply disappeared without issue" (484). Meltzer does believe, however, that the Clovis groups (to which the East Wenatchee group belongs) represent a successful cultural group in the Americas, and that the Colville and Yakama probably represent descendant groups.

Another alternative proposed by Joseph Greenberg, Christy Turner, and Stephen Zegura was that the North American continent was settled by three migrations—the first about 11,000 years ago, and the other two after 5,000 years ago (1986: 479–80). Even though numerous authors disagree with some or all of the evidence and conclusions reached in the Greenberg, Turner, and Zegura article (488–92), the possibility exists that the Wenatchee and Yakama are related to those groups who first came into the area 11,000 years ago.

Gramly, however, did outline procedures he would follow should scientific evidence show that human remains from the site (if any) were American Indian. He wrote:

> If in the course of biochemical and standard (traditional) quantitative studies, the East Wenatchee Clovis site human remains are deemed "American Indian," then the BMS [Buffalo Museum of Science] is willing to discuss the issue of reburial with concerned Native Americans. The Principal Investigator is sympathetic with advocates of respectful treatment of the dead. The BMS and Principal Investigator are not opposed to reburial of human remains that have been collected for scientific purposes. (1990: 16–17)

The Colville and other individuals protested the excavations in a peaceful protest on Monday, October 22. Gramly met the Indians through a locked gate wearing a bulletproof vest. The following day he, the landowner, representatives of the Colville tribe, and other officials met and reached an agreement (signed November 2) that called for him to complete the removal of the seventeen exposed artifacts, excavate the geological trench, notify the tribe in the event additional artifacts were encountered, called for the establishment of an advisory panel to develop a management plan for the site and all artifacts from it, called for Gramly to allow the tribe to appoint someone to monitor the excavations, and for an inventory of all the artifacts in the possession of the permittee.

A similar meeting was held with the Yakama, although no formal plan was developed. (According to Gramly's letter of February 23, 1991, however, a plan was developed, but the Yakama never signed it; therefore it never went into effect.)

Ultimately, no human remains were encountered, and no further problems were forthcoming. Gramly had agreed to the compromise, he said, because of the educational importance of the site. A large number of school children had been scheduled to tour the site, and their safety was his concern. "Gramly said his choice was either to dig under Indian protest with tours shut down or do a restricted dig with tours. He has said if one child who viewed the site becomes an archeologist because of it, the tours will have been worth it" (Wheat 1990h: 7).

GRAMLY AND THE ARCHAEOLOGISTS

The basis for the conflict within the archaeological community is apparently centered within a letter written to Mehringer from Richey in October 1988. This letter outlined conditions to be placed on the excavations, among them that the artifacts would not be destructively altered without Richey's permission, that the artifacts be kept on WSU premises and not taken outside without approval, that there be no casts made without prior approval, and that the artifacts be returned to Richey prior to the onset of new excavations (Gramly 1991). Waldorf also provides a short discussion of the reasons for Richey's "falling out with Pete Mehringer" (1991a: 2).

Specifically, the trouble between Gramly and the archaeologists of Washington seems to have been centered around the ultimate disposition of the artifacts.

> Mehringer said he wants to get the artifacts into public trust and that Richey's reluctance to make such a commitment was part of the problem between them. . . . Without a commitment to place the artifacts in public trust, WSU has been reluctant to continue the dig for fear it would be using taxpayers' money to gather a collection that then could be sold for Richey's profit. (Wheat 1990a: 2)

More basically, however, the conflict revolved around the broader issue of ethics—"the issue that came up . . . was the ethical issue. We [the Colville] felt ethics is a different issue" (Wheat 1990g: 1).

The circulation of copies of *Indian Artifact Magazine*, a quarterly publication for collectors of Indian artifacts, for which Gramly has written, brought up the discussion of ethics. "The magazine is 'offensive', and certainly casts serious questions as to his motives in this whole thing', said Colville tribal leader Dale Kohler" (Wren 1990b: 2); archaeologist Jerry Galm stated "'There are serious ethical questions here, and everyone wants to know why the rush—and that includes the Colville Confederated Tribes'" (Wren 1990b: 2). Ken Reid, also from WSU, said he "was concerned about going ahead with a dig when all regional archaeologists agreed preservation of the site was best" (Wheat 1990b: 2).

Gramly called this criticism "sour grapes" and the result of "'small minded, insular people' who lost the opportunity to dig through a 'falling out with Richey'" (Wren 1990b: 7).

Most of the archaeologists in Washington State were disappointed when the plans for the excavation were announced. Gramly had written to Mehringer

> to offer you and your students access to the specimens to be removed in 1990. There are many nondestructive studies that could be carried out on the pieces such as edge wear analyses. Provided the work is done on premises . . . I would welcome researchers from WSU. . . . Let me extend an invitation to you and your students to collect whatever soil samples you need to amplify the fine work you did in 1988. (Wheat 1990b: 2)

Mehringer did not respond to Gramly, primarily because, in his mind, he felt that "[t]he real question is the disposition of artifacts and the conduct of excavations" (Wheat 1990b: 2), and he would not be a part of excavations where the question was still in doubt.

In reality, the problem became blown out of proportion because of the extreme media attention focused on the site; both archaeologists and Gramly were at fault.

Gramly's application for the excavation permit, submitted in March 1990, was vague relative to the disposition of the artifacts. It presented six alternatives for the treatment of the artifacts:

1. donated to an accredited museum;
2. placed on permanent loan in a museum;
3. sold privately or publicly, the purchaser(s) being known—not anonymous;
4. sold to a foundation, the name of the foundation being known;
5. given to individuals or foundations, their name being known; or
6. held by the Richey family and its heirs. (Gramly 1990)

Early efforts at minimizing the conflict were not successful. In a September 26 proposal, Bruce Huckell of the Arizona State Museum called for a moratorium on excavation, and also suggested the formation of an advisory committee, made up of Paleo-Indian scholars from across the nation. This proposal was endorsed by Mehringer, Vance Haynes, George Frison, and the Colville. Gramly wrote to Huckell saying he would consider the moratorium, but that its suggestion was late in relation to the proposed excavation timetable (Wheat 1990a: 2). In spite of Frison's statement that "'[w]e should be a community of scholars rather than a bunch of people sniping at each other'" (1990a: 2), nothing ever came from the suggested moratorium.

Ultimately, the excavation went on, and the question about the disposition of the artifacts was not immediately resolved. The controversy did not end, however.

The landowner, Richey, began to get "fed up with dig squabbles" and "fed up with controversy over whether the dig . . . should continue" (Wheat 1990d: 2). Eventually, Richey failed to continue protecting the site with concrete slabs—he even planted apple trees in the site location. Gramly placed the blame on the situation:

All of us knew this man [Richey] wanted it dug. . . . To keep it undug was to risk losing it. It was held hostage. Ask Adeline Fredin [Colville tribal historian] or [Councilman] Mathew Dick [Jr.] or [archaeologist] Jerry Galm, or [archaeologist James] Chatters how they feel. They are the ones responsible in great measure for the events that have occurred. (Wheat 1990h: 7)

(For a different perspective on the conflict, read "Finding the Pony," by D. C. Waldorf [1991a: 2–4].)

In 1991, several groups began proceedings to purchase the site, including the state of Washington, the Pacific Northwest Archaeological Society, and John McKendry, a trustee for the Buffalo Museum of Science.

Jeff Mangel, president of the Pacific Northwest Archaeological Society, was quoted as saying that the society was attempting to preserve the public domain but also to protect the right of tribes to artifacts in their traditional lands: "If the society buys the property, and assuming we sign an agreement with the Colville people, the artifacts (from a future dig) will be the strict property of the Colville tribes" (Wheat 1991a: 2).

McKendry, however, had a different feeling entirely. His offer of $485,000 for the site was made on behalf of the Buffalo Museum of Science, and his aims did not appear to be as benign regarding the Colville: "If we dug it and got new artifacts, we would end up with them, and it would be our discretion what happened to them. . . . We'd bargain with Mack [Richey] for the rest, and they would probably end up at our museum" (Wheat 1991b: 2).

In reaction to McKendry, Mathew Dick of the Colville replied: "The Colville tribe has said that for many years it has watched the desecration of its grave sites in the name of progress and thirst for knowledge. I still believe there has to be a balance between the thirst for knowledge of our past and the sacredness of our burial grounds" (Wheat 1991b: 2).

Working under the assumption that the site would be purchased by the Pacific Northwest Archaeological Society, an agreement was signed on May 2, 1991, between the society and the Colville Confederated Tribes intending to cover future work on tribal and aboriginal lands. The Colville recognized that: "archeology on tribal lands can be beneficial both to the public domain and to the tribes insofar as such research may serve to substantiate, or in some cases add new dimensions to, the tribes' oral tradition" (Wheat 1991c: 11).

The main principles in the agreement reached by the two parties cover the paths of future research at the site, and included agreements that:

- the society would reach an agreement with the Colville prior to application for a dig permit, with the possibility that any excavation could be turned into a joint project with the tribe;
- the society would train tribal members in archaeology, while the Colville pledge to share information about their heritage as they deem appropriate;
- the society recognized tribal sovereignty over burials and that human remains and associated funerary items are sacred regardless of their antiquity and should be treated with utmost respect and reverence;
- the society would not pursue a dig containing human remains unless directed to do so by the Colville, and would cease

digging and seek direction if it encounters evidence of human remains;

- all artifacts recovered during joint digs would be property of the Colville for preservation and display;
- the society would get up to two years for scientific research and testing, with tests that alter the structure of the artifact done only with tribal permission;
- the society would assist the Colville in urging private owners to adhere to the principles, including giving artifacts to the Colville;
- the society would not charge admission to view a site unless necessary to support a dig or educational program;
- neither party would sanction a project that is not under the direction of at least one trained, professional archaeologist capable of performing research consistent with the highest standards of the profession;
- the society pledged to adhere to all tribal, state, and federal laws during a dig and subsequent research; and
- both parties agreed to encourage appropriate celebrations that they agree are necessary to build respect for the heritage left by the first Americans.

Pacific Northwest Archaeological Society president Mangel said that they were "glad to sign what hopefully will become a landmark agreement. . . . We felt it was time to codify a system of ethics for digs" (Wheat 1991e: 2).

Ultimately, an agreement was reached for the purchase of the site by the Pacific Northwest Archaeological Society for an amount believed to be around $500,000, with the state of Washington paying $250,000 for the artifact collection recovered during excavations (Wheat 1991g: 12). Gramly was pleased at the acquisition, stating, "We were in it for the science. We don't want to keep them [the artifacts] permanently in Buffalo and never have" (Wheat 1991g: 12).

Although a great deal of ink was used trying to place the blame, much of the controversy could have been sidestepped early on.

Gramly's failure to involve the Colville in the early aspects of the permit application led to the problems in that arena. It would have been easier to have formed an agreement for inclusion in the application; even if no agreement could be reached, documentation of the attempt would have strengthened his case. Because of this problem, science was indeed politicized. The question about human remains proved to be a moot point, but, had Gramly not antagonized the local American Indian groups, perhaps the entire five-by-seven meters originally proposed would have been excavated.

In relation to the disposition of the artifacts, nothing incorrect or unethical is apparent. Both parties were ethically correct in relationship to their personal viewpoints and professional stances, and both maintained their stances in a consistent manner throughout the issue.

Mehringer was correct in refusing to excavate the site, using public monies, when it was uncertain that the artifacts would be placed in public trust. He would have been unethical to do so. Gramly, however, was not under any such constraints. His excavations were totally and completely privately funded, and the disposition of the artifacts, after scientific study, is no different than returning artifacts to any other landowner upon completion of a privately funded dig. Scientific data were collected (although information from the site is not available at this time) in a manner that appears to have been consistent with scientific study of other sites.

At no time were Gramly's qualifications questioned (at least the questions did not appear in print): George Frison was quoted as saying, "Gramly is a perfectly well qualified archeologist" (Wheat 1990a: 2). It was Gramly's association with the *Indian Artifact Magazine*, and the purported sale of artifacts, that led to the question of ethics.

Gramly admitted:

I have occasionally purchased and sold artifacts, historic and prehistoric, ethnographic and archeological, off and on since I was 10-1/2 years old. . . . I do not ascribe to Article II of the SAA [Society for American Archaeology] bylaws [discouraging commercialism in archaeology] and for that reason have not been a member of the SAA for years. (Wheat 1990c: 2)

In response to this, Frison said "He's in the museum business, and museums buy and sell artifacts all the time. I can't believe Gramly would be out there selling artifacts for profit. I don't think he's that kind of person" (Wheat 1990c: 2).

Ethically, Gramly did nothing that was in conflict with the apparent personal value system under which he operated.

Where did the problem lie? An analysis of comments present in interviews published in the *Wenatchee World* and *Spokane Chronicle* indicate that the groups involved were all concerned about the excavation, but they all failed to communicate effectively with each of the other groups.

Gramly's primary problem, it may be suggested, is that he fails to hold the view that American Indian concerns with the scientific excavation of *all* archaeological sites are valid. He writes:

> I feel that no native American group has the right to dictate anything to any private property owner. Of course, with regard to graves and ceremonial sites, they (and anyone else) may wish to object to procedures. In a free society such expressions of opinion are allowable.
>
> Where an archaeological site can be linked unquestionably to an ethnic group, then it is ethical and humane that the group should have a voice in the alteration, exploration or development of such a site.
>
> Regarding very ancient remains, such as Clovis, no group can make a special claim that supersedes the claim of another group. An archaeologist working at a Clovis site has a right, just like any other person (whether native American or not), to express an opinion and has an equal voice in such matters. (1991)

Most archaeologists probably agree that extremely old material cannot be assigned to existing ethnic groups. Joseph C. Winter asks: "Should we always respond positively to Native Americans, just because they are 'Indians'?" (1980: 126). Additionally, Lawrence Rosen questions: "Who has the right to excavate, or prevent the excavation of, a recent or ancient burial site, and on what authority is that right to be based?" (1980: 6). Is there something inherently "better" about a recommendation from an American Indian than a recommendation offered by any other individual, including a scientist?

In the state of Washington, the local archaeologists have developed an excellent working relationship with the Colville and other local groups through communication about all archaeological sites located on the aboriginal lands (at time of Euroamerican contact) of the native populations. Such an agreement between the Pacific Northwest Archaeological Society and the Colville may work for archaeologists in the state of Washington, but it may not work elsewhere.

Gramly's failure to involve the Colville and the Yakama may have cost him and archaeology valuable data about some of the earliest inhabitants of the North American continent.

In summation, all of the involved groups were equally at fault concerning the handling of the excavations at the East Wenatchee Clovis site in 1990. And because of miscommunication and the way that the problem was played out through the media rather than in group discussions, science may have been lost.

The only group that appears to have won what they set out to win are the Colville—they got the site "protected" from excavation without tribal involvement. The Yakama still have a resolution opposing the dig at the Richey cache (Wheat 1991f).

Ultimately, the question will have to deal with the ethics of how archaeologists handle archaeological remains. Better working agreements between archaeologists and local ethnic groups (not just American Indians) will need to be developed. These local groups should be included in discussions regarding archaeological sites found on their native lands, especially when those sites are probably related to their groups.

At this point, we know very little about why the Clovis group stopped at the East Wenatchee Clovis site. Mehringer believes that, "judging from the artifact assemblage, an unusual ceremony—most likely interment of an important person—is more probable than a hunt" (1989: 30). Gramly believes that the pieces of bone found at the site may be sled runners, and that sleds may have been used to cover the artifact pit, which contained the Clovis points (Wheat 1991d, 1991g). We may never know anything more about the site than the bare minimum. The radar anomaly recorded in 1988 that lies adjacent to (east of) unit 8 might hold the answer, but we may never know.

CONCLUSIONS

The problem . . . is not a clash of good and evil, ignorance and wisdom: it is a conflict between propositions that must be accorded equal moral weight from the outset. (Rosen 1980: 17)

In the past, American Indian groups were fragmented, played one against the other by various governmental, tribal, or societal groups; at the East Wenatchee Clovis site, the opposite appears to be true— the scientific community became fragmented and appeared disorganized.

The issues involved in the conflict extend beyond the excavation of a single Paleo-Indian cache. Even though the problem was fought out in the state of Washington, there are implications to archaeology nationwide.

The ultimate repercussions may center around the facts that:

1. the Colville have essentially been able to extend tribal control (on a religious or social basis) back in time over 11,000 years;
2. at least on a statewide level (and perhaps nationwide), precedent has been set that *may* require consultation with *any* American Indian group that decides to test the discipline;
3. excavations on private land (with private retention of artifact ownership) were controlled by a governmental agency;
4. archaeologists were divided in their reaction to what may be perceived to be a threat to the "resource," with one group allied with "outsiders" against a member of the discipline;
5. the issue at the core of the conflict was not "scientific," but "ethical"; the questions did not center around the science of archaeology (as a discipline), but the ethics of an archaeologist (as an individual);
6. there were no truly ethical differences, only differences in ethical systems; and
7. intradiscipline squabbles were carried out in the public media, rather than in the scientific media.

In spite of the seemingly harmonious end to this situation, archaeologists and American Indians of the state of Washington were to encounter another situation that would again focus the attention of the archaeological and nonarchaeological world on the region— the discovery of the "Ancient One," more commonly called "Kennewick Man."

9

⚬⌒⚬⋈⚬⌒⚬

"The Ancient One" of Kennewick

This first half of this chapter is a chronological reckoning of the events that have transpired so far; the latter half is an analysis of the situation as it relates to the conflict between American Indians and archaeologists.

It does not seem likely that the two individuals walking along the Columbia River in July 1996 understood the impact their Sunday afternoon at the hydroplane races would have on archaeology and the question of human origins in the new world. Perhaps, had they or any of the primary players in the saga involving the "Ancient One" (or "Kennewick Man") known what the impact would be, someone might have suggested that the material be left where it was and let well enough alone.

However, that was not the case. On Sunday, July 28, 1996, Will Thomas and Dave Deacy stumbled across a human skull eroding out of the banks of the Columbia River near Kennewick, Washington. The Benton County coroner, Floyd Johnson, called forensic anthropologist James Chatters for a consultation. Upon examination, Chatters determined the skull was not from a murder victim, exhibited worn teeth indicative of precontact Indians, and was of a color more commonly associated with relatively old cultural material. Following a visit to the site of discovery, Chatters ultimately was able to recover an almost entire skeleton from the area.

135

The following day, Chatters and Johnson began the task of determining the age, sex, cultural background, and antiquity of the materials. If analyses determined that the material represented the remains of a Native American individual, then the material would fall under the Native American Graves Protection and Repatriation Act (NAGPRA) of 1990. The characteristics of the human skull led Chatters to believe that the remains came from a male individual, between forty and fifty-five years old, about five feet nine inches tall, and "Caucasoid." Chatters's idea was that the individual was probably "an early pioneer or fur trapper" (Preston 1997: 70).

A CAT scan of the pelvis revealed a stone projectile point tip of the type thought to be approximately 4,500 to 9,000 years old. On August 5, at the coroner's request, the left fifth metacarpal was sent to the University of California at Riverside for radiocarbon testing. The sample returned a date of between 9,200 and 9,600 years ago, and, once the antiquity of the bones was tentatively established, the Corps of Engineers, citing NAGPRA as authority for its actions, halted all analysis. On September 2, 1996, they took possession of the remains and had them placed in a vault at the Pacific Northwest National Laboratory in Richland, Washington.

As an "Inadvertent Discovery" under NAGPRA, the corps determined that it was obligated to notify the American Indian tribes "likely to be culturally affiliated with" the remains, that aboriginally occupied the area, or upon whose lands (or aboriginal homelands) the materials were found and to initiate consultation regarding the ultimate disposition of the remains.

On September 9, as a result of the consultation initiated by the Corps of Engineers, five tribal groups (the Umatilla, the Yakama, the Nez Perce, the Colville, and the Wanapum) filed a joint claim for the human remains. Armand Minthorn, a Umatilla religious leader (and later NAGPRA Review Committee member), in a tribal position paper published by the *Tri-City Herald* on October 27, 1996, wrote:

> If this individual is truly over 9,000 years old, that only substantiates our belief that he is Native American. From our oral histories, we know that our people have been part of this land since the beginning of time. . . .
>
> Some scientists say that if this individual is not studied further, we, as Indians, will be destroying evidence of our own history. We already

know our history. It is passed on to us through our elders and through our religious practices. (Minthorn 1996)

The Corps of Engineers published a "Notice of Intent to Repatriate" in the September 17 and 24, 1996, editions of the *Tri-City Herald* (a local newspaper). But on October 16, before the mandatory thirty-day waiting period had expired, eight scientists filed suit in the district court to block the proposed repatriation. These eight scientists—Robson Bonnichsen, C. Loring Brace, George W. Gill, C. Vance Haynes Jr., Richard L. Jantz, Douglas Owsley, Dennis J. Stanford, and D. Gentry Steele—are some of the major figures in the field of American anthropology dealing with the initial peopling of the Americas. The lawsuit filed by the group forced the corps to halt plans to repatriate the material until the court could decide on the merits of the plaintiffs' case.

At issue was the corps's determination that the material was "Native American," and therefore subject to repatriation under NAGPRA. Secondly, while NAGPRA allows the scientific study of materials when the outcome would be of "major benefit to the United States" (45 CFR Part 10.10[c][1]), the scientists argued that the corps's intent to repatriate was infringing on their civil rights to study the remains simply because they were not "Native American" (*Bonnichsen v. United States*, USDC CV No. 96-1481-JE, filed October 16, 1996).

Other individuals in the area filed "symbolic" claims to the remains in order to prevent their reburial prior to study (Stang 1996). Additionally, the Asatru Folk Assembly, a California-based organization following an Old Norse religion, filed a similar complaint against the corps, alleging that, if the individual was "Caucasian" and in North America 8,400 years ago, they might also be culturally affiliated with the remains (Horn 1997: 511).

On February 3, 1997, U.S. magistrate John Jelderks refused to throw out the lawsuits filed by the scientists and the Asatru Folk Assembly. On March 23, the corps rescinded its decision to return the remains to the tribes under NAGPRA (Lee 1997a).

During the preliminary oral arguments heard by Magistrate Jelderks on June 2, 1997, in the U.S. District Court for the District of Oregon, the scientists requested immediate access to the remains. Magistrate Jelderks issued a written opinion with the intent "to supplement and amplify... bench rulings, and to provide additional guidance to the defendants so that this controversy may be resolved in a timely and orderly manner" (Jelderks 1997: 3). While the court's primary issue revolved around the determination of whether or not the remains are subject to NAGPRA, it also outlined sixteen other issues that it felt the corps should consider:

1. what is meant by terms such as "Native American" and "indigenous" in the context of NAGPRA;
2. whether . . . NAGPRA applies to remains or cultural objects from a population that failed to survive and is not directly related to modern Native Americans;
3. whether NAGPRA requires . . . a *biological* connection between the remains and a contemporary Native American tribe;
4. whether there has to be any *cultural* affiliation between the remains and a contemporary Native American tribe;
5. the level of certainty required to establish such biological or cultural affiliation;
6. whether any scientific studies are needed before the corps can determine whether these particular remains are subject to NAGPRA;
7. whether there is evidence of a link, either biological or cultural, between the remains and a modern Native American tribe or to any other ethnic or cultural group;
8. whether the study provisions of 25 USC 3005(b) are limited to objects that were in the possession or control of a federal agency or museum prior to November 16, 1990;
9. whether there is any other law . . . or any other section of NAGPRA . . . that either permits or forbids scientific study of these remains;
10. whether scientific study and repatriation of the remains are mutually exclusive;
11. what law controls if the remains are not subject to NAGPRA;
12. what happens to the remains if no existing tribe can establish a cultural affiliation;
13. whether plaintiffs have a right . . . to study the remains;
14. whether there is any merit to the contention of the *Asatru* plaintiffs that non-Indians should be permitted to file a claim to the remains;

15. what role ... the NAGPRA Review Committee should play in resolving the issue presented by this case; and

16. whether NAGPRA is silent on important issues raised by this case, and whether congressional action will be required to clarify the law regarding "culturally unidentifiable ancient remains." (Jelderks 1997: 45–51)

In an article published in the July 16, 1997, issue of the *Tri-City Herald*, reporter Mike Lee stated that the U.S. Senate was "expected to approve a bill this morning that encourages the Army Corps of Engineers to be an 'impartial party' in determining" the future of the Kennewick remains. The Energy and Water Development Appropriations Bill contained an amendment offered by Washington state Republican senator Slade Gordon that argued that "information providing greater insight into American prehistory should be collected, preserved, and disseminated for the benefit of the country as a whole" (quoted in Lee 1997b).

In late August, Washington State University (WSU) anthropology professor Gary Huckleberry applied to the Corps of Engineers to conduct archaeological testing at the site where the human remains were found in order to obtain additional information, and, on October 31, the corps agreed to allow Huckleberry to participate in additional testing.

Subsequent to Huckleberry's test excavations, one of Washington's representatives to the U.S. House of Representatives, "Doc" Hastings, introduced a bill that would amend NAGPRA and allow anthropologists access to study such "culturally unaffiliated" human remains as Kennewick Man. The bill, House Resolution 2893, introduced into Congress on November 7, 1997, would, according to Richard Jantz, "make it much easier for (scientists) to gain study access to any unaffiliated material, and it will require that (cultural) affiliation be documented to a much greater extent" (quoted in Lee 1997c: 5). But National Congress of American Indians general counsel John Dosset felt Hastings's proposed law would place "scientific study in a place of greater importance than the protection of the graves of Indian ancestors" (quoted in Lee 1997c: 5).

Sampling of the discovery site began on Saturday, December 13, by a "team" of corps and WSU scientists and other researchers appointed by the Confederated Tribes of the Umatilla Reservation (Lee 1997d). Excavations confirmed the presence of volcanic ash believed to have been deposited by the eruption of Mount Mazama in southwestern Oregon approximately 6,800 years ago.

Shortly after the completion of the testing of the site, the Corps of Engineers received a letter from the National Park Service departmental consulting archaeologist Francis P. McManamon that provided guidance to the agency in response to the questions of Magistrate Jelderks's opinion of June 2, 1997. In this letter, McManamon responded that there was insufficient information to determine whether or not the remains were subject to NAGPRA, but provided two questions that, if answered in the positive, would subject the remains to NAGPRA. It provided information relative to the questioned definitions of "Native American" and "indigenous" in the context of NAGPRA, applying NAGPRA to "all tribes, peoples and cultures that occupied the United States prior to historically documented European exploration" (McManamon 1997: 3). It stated that NAGPRA did not *require* a biological connection between human remains found on federal or tribal lands and an Indian tribe that requested the repatriation of the remains. Additionally, McManamon stated that scientific studies may be carried out "if there is a concern as to whether the human remains in question are Native American within the meaning of NAGPRA," and that there is "nothing in NAGPRA, its implementing regulations or other Federal law [that] precludes analysis of human remains or cultural items excavated or discovered on Federal or tribal land . . . for the purpose of determining whether those remains or items are Native American within the meaning of NAGPRA" (5). However, McManamon went on to recommend that any additional studies be conducted in consultation with Indian tribes and other interested parties.

In a January 3, 1998, edition of the *Tri-City Herald*, the Corps of Engineers announced plans to cover the Kennewick Man site. The plans, initially suggested in October 1997, called for the corps to bury the area with approximately four feet of rock dropped by helicopter as well as the planting of willow trees across the site (Lee 1998a). Ten days later, Senator Gorton and Representative Hastings asked the corps to reconsider its plan to cover the site. The corps continued to maintain that "protection" of the area was necessary, even while the two Washington politicians requested the decision be reviewed. On Tuesday, March 17, a provision tucked into the U.S. Senate Appropriations Committee emergency supplemental budget blocked the corps from taking the action they proposed to "protect" the site where the Kennewick remains were found.

The situation heated up when, on March 19, the Advisory Council on Historical Preservation agreed to the Corps of Engineers' determination that burying the site would have "no adverse effect." Washington State archaeologist Robert Whitlam also agreed that the corps's offered plan would have "no adverse effect" on the property. In a court brief filed Wednesday, March 18, corps lawyers said they intended to implement the plan on March 24, 1998, or as soon as they would be able to obtain approval from all agencies necessary (Lee 1998b). On Wednesday, March 25, the corps announced it had awarded a $160,000 contract to cover about 250 feet of shoreline with rocks and dirt in an effort to "ward off erosion and bone hunters" (Lee 1998c). On Thursday, March 26, the U.S. Senate passed a rider attached to a disaster relief bill that would prevent the corps from burying the Kennewick Man site.

Hastings introduced H.R. 3575 into Congress on March 17, 1998, "to preserve the integrity of the Kennewick Man remains for scientific study, and for other purposes." Section 1 of the bill also constrained the secretary of the army from stabilizing covering, or permanently altering the site where Kennewick Man was found until after the disposition of the *Bonnichsen* court case. On Tuesday, March 31, after Hastings contacted the corps, the project was put on hold. But on Monday, April 6, rock and dirt were dropped onto the site where the remains of the skeleton known as "Kennewick Man" was found.

The site had been buried, but Department of the Interior involvement in the conflict continued to escalate when it announced that tests on the skeletal material were being planned. At the same time, representatives of Hastings's office confirmed that they would continue to press for the passage of H.R. 2893 originally introduced in November 1997.

With the closure of the site from which the bones were recovered, attention turned to the bones themselves. The U.S. Department of Justice requested that the University of California at Davis return the fragments of bone from Kennewick Man in the university's

possession, indicating that such materials were government property. Scientists at the university, however, were hesitant to turn over
such items, citing the desire to protect the scientific integrity of the
materials. The government allowed the school to retain the sample,
but refused to allow continuation of DNA studies. Ultimately, the
Justice Department recovered the sample from the laboratory in
February 1999.

Another question concerning the bones was brought out when it
was learned that corps officials had given a rib fragment recovered
in December 1997 (not from the original collection made by Chatters in 1996) to the Confederated Tribes of the Umatilla Indian Reservation, who reburied the material on April 27. While the material inadvertently given to the tribe was not housed within the same
area where the bulk of the Kennewick remains were housed, it did
raise questions about the safety of the bones. Magistrate Jelderks
issued a court order on May 13 that noted "a succession of incidents
and disclosures during the preceding months has raised serious
questions concerning both the physical security and scientific integrity of the human remains" (quoted in Bradford 1998). On May
28, the court ordered that the skeletal material be moved from the
Pacific Northwest National Laboratory in Richland, Washington,
to a place agreed upon by all parties in the case. On August 31,
Magistrate Jelderks ordered the material transferred to the Burke
Museum at the University of Washington in Seattle. An inventory
originally proposed for September was finally begun in October, immediately prior to the transfer of the bones to the Burke Museum.
On Thursday, October 29, the containers of bone containing the
skeletal remains arrived at the Burke.

On Wednesday, July 1, the Department of the Interior, which had
taken over authority of the bones from the Corps of Engineers, introduced a new wrinkle in the case. Initially, the corps had been
proceeding from the viewpoint that the material had been found
on aboriginal lands of various tribes, but the Interior Department
report to the court emphasized that the lands upon which the remains were found were *not* from a location "within any area recognized as the aboriginal land of any Indian tribe in a final judgment of the Indian Claims Commission or the United States Court
of Federal Claims" (quoted in Lee 1998d).

Also on July 1, the Interior Department submitted a draft plan to
study the skeletal remains, with an inventory of the bones in Sep-

tember, and tests beginning in November. Among the tests proposed were: an inventory of the bones and teeth; an analysis of the stone point embedded in the pelvis; scientific measurements of the skull and teeth; and an overall assessment of the physical characteristics of the skeleton. If none of these tests indicate a cultural link to modern people, the government proposed utilizing additional radiocarbon dating and DNA extraction. The plaintiff scientists complained that the plan was too vague and that the radiocarbon and DNA tests should be performed as a matter of course and not only if the cultural link was tenuous or unproven.

On February 10, 1999, the Justice Department announced plans for the tests proposed by Interior Department scientists. The tests, to be run between February 25 and March 5, were to be conducted by a team of five scientists—Gary Huckleberry (who participated in the December 1997 study of the Kennewick site) to study the sediments attached to the bones; John Fagan to study the stone point embedded in Kennewick Man's pelvis; Joseph Powell to study the teeth and cranium; Julie Stein to study the sediments and geoarchaeology of the Kennewick Man site; and Jerome Rose to study the bones and teeth. The limited study, while not as detailed as those proposed by the eight plaintiff scientists, was aimed at gathering information to help the government decide whether the remains should be repatriated to the American Indians who had filed the repatriation claims.

The reports, filed in mid-April, were finally made available to the public on October 14, 1999. The resulting publication of the reports, entitled *Report on the Non-Destructive Examination, Description, and Analysis of the Human Remains from Columbia Park, Kennewick, Washington*, on the analysis of the Kennewick material has four chapters: chapter 1, "The Initial Scientific Examination, Description, and Analysis of the Kennewick Man Human Remains" by Francis P. McManamon; chapter 2, "Report on the Osteological Assessment of the 'Kennewick Man' Skeleton (CENWW.97.Kennewick)" by Joseph F. Powell and Jerome C. Rose; chapter 3, "Analysis of Sediments Associated with Human Remains Found at Columbia Park, Kennewick, WA" by Gary Huckleberry and Julie K. Stein; and chapter 4, "Analysis of Lithic Artifact Embedded in the Columbia Park Remains" by John L. Fagan.

McManamon's chapter "describes the administrative, legal, and regulatory background for the government's investigation of the

Kennewick remains" (McManamon 1999: 1), but, more importantly, it stated that the Interior Department was "attempting to demonstrate that NAGPRA is flexible enough to allow good science to go forward at the same time respecting the dignity and recognizing the importance of traditional tribal beliefs" (2). It also provides a general summary of the studies and results of the other three chapters of the report.

In describing the results of the nondestructive phase of the research, McManamon notes that the investigation was not adequate to establish whether the remains were "Native American" for the purposes of NAGPRA because of insufficient chronological information that could be obtained without destructive analysis. He also notes that the physical appearance of the remains, with the absence of any scavenger marks on the bones, suggests that they were quickly buried at death—although the method of burial, whether cultural or natural, is not known.

The chapter by Powell and Rose details the techniques used in refitting the parts of the body and the measurements taken by the scientists to make their analyses. Of these analyses and comparisons, the authors were only able to assert, based on the craniometric data (measurements made on the skull), that the individual known as Kennewick Man does not fit within any of the samples derived from a "modern or recent human population indigenous to the Americas" (Powell and Rose 1999: 11) and that "the Kennewick skeleton morphologically is unlike any modern human population" (14). Additionally, their research showed that there is at least some morphological similarity between Kennewick and Archaic groups within the United States, although the Archaic populations from the southeastern United States are clearly distinct (16).

Ultimately, Powell and Rose conclude that "the Kennewick individual is unique relative to recent American Indians, and finds its closest association with groups of Polynesia and the Ainu of Japan" (1999: 19), and that the skeleton "can be excluded, on the basis of dental and cranial morphology, from recent American Indians. More importantly, it can be excluded (on the basis of typicality probabilities) from *all* late Holocene human groups" (20, emphasis in original).

The summary of the information from the skeletal material, the sediments from which the material came, and the projectile point embedded in the hip portion of the skeleton provided the basic documentation required under the Archaeological Resources Protection Act (ARPA) and NAGPRA, but it also pointed out the need for additional testing. It detailed why additional radiocarbon dates were requested in September 1999, when two pieces of bone were selected and divided into samples for submission to three different radiocarbon laboratories—Beta Analytical of Miami, Florida; NSF–Arizona AMS Facility at the University of Arizona in Tucson, Arizona; and the University of California, Riverside, Radiocarbon Laboratory, in Riverside, California (McManamon 1999: 10).

Following the results of the radiocarbon dating, McManamon noted that the next step by the Interior Department would be to undertake further studies to help determine the ultimate disposition of the remains if they were found to be Native American, as defined by NAGPRA.

Once the remains were reasonably determined to be "Native American," then further tests were scheduled to help determine "cultural affiliation," defined by NAGPRA as "a relationship of shared group identity which can reasonably be traced historically or prehistorically between members of a present-day Indian tribe . . . and an identifiable earlier group" (43 CFR Part 10.2[e]).

In early January 2000 (Lee 2000a), four experts were chosen to help establish the links between Kennewick Man and American Indian groups: Eugene Hunn of the University of Washington (linguistics); Steven Hackenberger of Central Washington University (bioarchaeology and mortuary archaeology); Kenneth Ames of Portland State University (archaeology); and Daniel Boxberger of Eastern Washington University (traditional history and ethnography).

When the results of the second round of radiocarbon testing supported the original date of Kennewick Man (Lee 2000b), the National Park Service announced its plans to submit material for DNA testing as a further possibility of determining the cultural affiliation of the remains (Lee 2000c). The tribes immediately criticized the plan as unnecessary and disturbing to them (Lee 2000d).

Throughout this struggle, Hastings continued to try to amend NAGPRA. On June 10, 1998, hearings on H.R. 2893 were held in Congress. Speakers testifying at the hearings included representatives of the Interior Department, the National Congress of American Indians, American Indian tribal leaders, the archaeological community, and other scientists. No further action was taken on the bill during the legislative session.

The testimony again seemed to reflect the schism between American Indians and scientists, as such, the government was opposed to the proposed bill. Katherine H. Stevenson, associate director of the National Park Services' Cultural Resource Stewardship and Partnerships program, spoke against the bill, offering that the stated goals of the bill would be better met through regulations and guidance rather than through legislation. She noted: "To reopen the law now could polarize the various interests affected by NAGPRA" (testimony before the House Resource Committee, June 10, 1998), a situation that might lead to more conflict between the parties.

No further action was taken on the bill during the session, but the desire by Hastings to amend NAGPRA did not diminish. Hastings reintroduced the bill as H.R. 2643 and, on July 29, 1999, it was again referred to the House Resource Committee.

ANALYSIS OF THE SITUATION

The happenings in Washington that have taken place as a result of the discovery of the human skeletal material offers some insight into the nature of the conflict between American Indians and archaeology. Certain features must be noted, particularly the roles of the popular press (as indicated by newspapers and popular magazines), the discipline of archaeology (as indicated by representatives of the Society for American Archaeology and the eight plaintiffs of the court case against the government), the government (as indicated by the Corps of Engineers and representatives of the National Park Service), and the legislative issues embroiled in the process.

AMERICAN INDIANS VERSUS AMERICAN ARCHAEOLOGISTS: SCIENTIFIC ISSUES

One of the primary issues in archaeology in the New World is the mechanism and antiquity of the initial peopling of the continent. The hunt for early "Americans" has driven many scientists throughout the late nineteenth and entire twentieth centuries. Again, as part of the study of the history of American archaeology, numerous authors have outlined the quest for early Americans, but perhaps the most detailed study has been compiled by David J. Meltzer (1983). Meltzer's work outlines not only the academic milieu in which this quest has taken place, but also the social milieu of the academy as the quest for the earliest Americans took place.

Throughout the development of North American archaeology, the question of not only "When did the first people get here?", but related questions such as "Where geographically did they come from?", "Where biologically did they come from?", and "How did they get here?" equally intrigued early practitioners. Once the idea that American Indians were responsible for all the sites in the New World was accepted, archaeologists struggled to develop chronologies upon which to construct the development of human habitation in North and South America.

With the development of scientific ideas concerning the Bering Strait land bridge and an ice-free corridor through the MacKenzie Mountains (see Fagan 1987; Shutler 1983), scientists thought they had the "how" and both "where" questions answered, but they continued to work on the "when."

Lanceolate projectile points associated with extinct mammoths in Clovis, New Mexico, became the oldest known complex of cultural material known in the New World and, with the development of radiocarbon dating in the 1950s, it was found to date to around 11,200 years old. The continuing refinements of dating techniques led scientists to believe that they would soon be able to pin down the earliest indications of people in North America. But even in 1989, authors were still asking "Why don't we know when the first people came to North America?" (Meltzer 1989: 471).

Since the early 1970s, excavations of archaeological sites (such as Meadowcroft rock shelter in Pennsylvania and Monte Verde in Chile, South America) that appeared to contain cultural material older than the established sequences and accepted dates for migration into the New World forced scientists to question more fully their theorems. With the acceptance of the age of Monte Verde in Chile (Meltzer et al. 1997: 659–63) at about 12,450 years ago, older than any previously known and accepted archaeological site in the New World, the "Clovis first" model of New World occupation was brought seriously under attack.

The Monte Verde material and the Meadowcroft material do not fit into preconceived notions of what the technology of the ancestors of the Clovis culture would look like. Nor, for that matter, had scientists been able to find an acceptable Old World ancestor for the Clovis material. If the oldest known site is in South America rather than in the far north, and if there are no recognizable cultural antecedents in the area from where the earliest immigrants were supposedly to have come, where did the first Americans come from, when did they arrive, and how did they get to the New World?

It was upon this unraveling scientific tapestry of New World archaeology that the discovery of Kennewick materials was cast.

Because of the external features of the skull, Chatters's suggestion that the material was probably related to an early homesteader in the area seemed likely, but there were ambiguities that caused some concern. Chatters said that despite the appearance of the skull, history suggested that it could not be too old since Lewis and Clark did not visit the area until 1805. "We might just have someone buried in the back yard of a homestead," he was quoted as saying (Schafer 1996).

But once the antiquity of the remains were established, the availability of a set of human remains that might offer information on lifestyles of early inhabitants of North America excited the scientific world and started a wave of curiosity by the world in general regarding the process by which early populations came into the North and South American continents. Two books have recently been published on the situation—Roger Downey's *Riddle of the Bones: Politics, Science, Race, and the Story of Kennewick Man* (2000) and David Hurst Thomas's *Skull Wars: Archaeology and the Search for Native American Identity* (2000). Articles published in such popular venues as *The New Yorker* (Preston 1997), the *U.S. News and World Report* (Petit 1998), *Discover* (Wright 1999), *Newsweek* (Begley and Murr 1999), and even the CBS television news program *Sixty Minutes* (Columbia Broadcasting System 1998), suggested the discovery could prove that the possible origins of American Indians lay either much further back in time or from a much different region in the Old World than previously expected.

From the beginning, the popular press misused and confused the word "Caucasoid" (as a descriptive term applied to certain biological features) with "Caucasian" (a culturally defined racial type).

Almost overnight, the location of the proposed founder populations for American Indians was magically transformed from the steppes of northeast Asia to the Caucasus region of southeast Europe—from "Mongolian" to "Caucasian," from "yellow" to "white."

This played well with the focus of such groups as the Asatru Folk Assembly, which attempted to assert a claim for early "colonization" of the New World by European populations, but it also intrigued scientists, for entirely different reasons. While the Asatru Folk Assembly claimed the remains as those of an "ancestor," scientists focused on them for their scientific value. Archaeologist Robson Bonnichsen was quoted as saying: "There's a whole book of information [in Kennewick Man's bones]. To put him back in the ground is like burning a rare book so we'll learn nothing. . . . It seems to be the case there is a major effort to block scientific inquiry into the study of American origins" (quoted in O'Hagan 1998: 8).

But American Indians were not amenable to further study. To representatives of the Umatilla, it did not matter how old the remains were. Additionally, Armand Minthorn noted: "Scientists have dug up and studied American Indians for decades. We view this practice as desecration of the body and a violation of our most deeply held religious beliefs. Our beliefs and policies also tell us this individual must be reburied as soon as possible" (1996).

With this stance, it was not likely that a compromise between scientists and American Indians could be reached. Minthorn addressed this issue also:

> Many people are asking if there's any chance for a compromise in this issue. We remind them that not only has this individual been compromised, but also our religions beliefs have once again been compromised. Many non-Indians are looking for a compromise— a compromise that fits their desires. (1996)

But Don Sampson, a former chairman for the Confederated Tribes of the Umatilla Indian Reservation's Board of Trustees, stated in a position paper for the Confederated Tribes of the Umatilla Indian Reservation:

> We want the public and scientists to understand that we do not reject science. In fact, we have anthropologists and other scientists on staff, and we use science every day to help in protecting our people

and the land. However, we do reject the notion that science is the answer to everything and therefore it should take precedence over the religious rights and beliefs of American citizens. (1997)

A year later, another group involved in the process reaffirmed the stance. Marla Big Boy, an attorney for the Colville Tribe, told reporters at a press conference in Santa Fe in December 1998: "The Colville Tribe is not against science. We are against the use of science to discriminate and disenfranchise Native American tribes" (quoted in Coleman 1998).

Thus, the question at the outset was not only a question of science versus religion, as some of the popular press reported, but also a conflict between American Indian philosophy and that of American science. And the scientists were not of a single mind in relation to their philosophy. Articles and letters in the American Anthropological Association's *Anthropology News* discussed the political and academic implications of Kennewick, especially in relation to the scientific and social definitions of "race."

With the publication of the results of the analyses on the skeletal material, it became obvious that science was facing the possibility of losing one of the "founder populations" of North America. The fact that the skeleton was not related to *any* recent human groups, especially any American Indian groups, makes it more difficult to justify repatriating it to any particular Indian group and easier to justify continued study.

The additional fact that the skeleton shows some resemblance to the Archaic populations of the United States, which temporally follows hints that the Archaic groups *may* have derived some of their morphological characteristics from the population of which the Kennewick individual was a member. Equally intriguing is the distinctiveness of the Archaic population of the southeastern United States from the western Archaic populations.

AMERICAN INDIANS VERSUS
AMERICAN ARCHAEOLOGISTS: LEGAL ISSUES

While conflicts between the scientific possibilities raised by the discovery of "The Ancient One" have been raised, the principle issue continues to be the legal question of whether NAGPRA should apply to materials of such antiquity.

Many individuals were quick to see the legal ramifications of the situation, and attorneys more often focused on the case law relating to human remains.

In 1997, Amanda Horn examined the legal issues surrounding NAGPRA and its application to the ancient human remains and the battle between archaeologists "for the right to control the disposition of human remains discovered on federal land in Washington" (1997: 503). Horn's examination focused on Congress's failure to recognize the religious relationship between cultural items (including human remains) and the tribes, the differences in application of certain state statutes regarding Native American human remains, as well as a history of the Kennewick discovery.

Horn then details the challenges to NAGPRA inherent in the eight anthropologists' court case against the Corps of Engineers: that is, that Congress did not contemplate remains as old as Kennewick in its enactment of NAGPRA, that modern tribes will not be able to demonstrate adequately a "cultural affiliation" with material as old as Kennewick, and that the corps's action to repatriate the material is unwarranted until further study allows an accurate determination of the Kennewick material's ethnicity and cultural affiliation (1997: 512). The archaeologists also relied upon the scientific exceptions provision of NAGPRA, which allows scientific testing of materials when the results would be of a major benefit to the U.S. government.

American Indian concerns with the human remains were also discussed. Horn argues that, strictly speaking, under NAGPRA, the Corps of Engineers must immediately repatriate the remains upon request to Native American tribal groups that can provide evidence of cultural affiliation (25 USC 3005[c]), which the tribes provided through oral histories, and also since the land upon which the remains were found are considered to be within the aboriginal homeland of the Columbia Basin tribes, based upon an 1855 treaty between the Umatilla and the federal government that secured hunting, fishing, gathering, and other rights to the Umatilla on their traditional homeland (1997: 513).

In relation to the scientific exception clause of NAGPRA, Horn's analysis illustrates what many Native Americans feel about the scientific study of human remains:

The scientists' arguments . . . are reduced to a belief that their interests in knowledge and education outweigh the religious, civil and sovereign rights of the Native Americans. . . . From the Native American perspective, the proposed compromise constitutes no compromise at all as the word is commonly defined. Instead, the compromise illustrates another example of the subordination of Native American ideals by the dominant power. (1997: 516)

CONCLUSIONS

In conclusion, Horn realizes that "the Kennewick man will probably be subjected to a complete scientific examination before he is released to a tribe for reburial" (1997: 516), that the disposition of the remains will "significantly impact decisions regarding the control of remains discovered in the future" (517), and also that "the discovery and the long journey that the Kennewick man will inevitably travel before being put to rest, solidifies a foundation for discussion between the Native Americans and archaeologists" (517).

Horn's analysis is an accurate assessment of the situation regarding Kennewick. At present, the future of the remains are uncertain. The scientific analyses that were permitted have failed to provide any additional information that would help the Interior Department in its decision concerning the disposition of the remains.

An additional point that Horn discusses but does not analyze is the status of the land upon which the human remains were located. While the land in question is within land that the 1855 treaty between the Umatilla and the federal government did secure as a portion of their traditional homeland (Horn 1997: 513), the report on the Non-Destructive Examination of the Kennewick remains states that Section 3(a)(2)(c) of NAGPRA (25 U.S.C. 3002[a][2][c]) does not apply because "a careful legal analysis of the judicial decisions by the Indian Land Claims Commission and the Court of Claims shows that the land where the remains were discovered has not been judicially determined to be the *exclusive* aboriginal territory of any modern tribe" (McManamon 1999: 2, emphasis added).

The court's decision will impact the disposition of human remains along at least two fronts: the application of NAGPRA to ancient remains, and the scientific exceptions clause.

If truly ancient remains such as those exemplified by the Kennewick material are excluded from protection or disposition under NAGPRA, the court will need to provide guidance on the age that human remains must be in order to be considered "ancient," as well as whether "science" or "tribal oral history" should be used to define that threshold. The NAGPRA Review Committee has partially addressed this issue but it has not yet been resolved.

Additionally, the court decision might also affect the scientific exception clause of NAGPRA, which allows for the scientific study of materials when the results of such is deemed to be of a major benefit to the U.S. government. The study of human remains of such antiquity will likely be deemed to be "of benefit to the United States," especially in relation to the information present regarding early peoples of the New World.

It must also be remembered that the court decision will be binding only in this judicial circuit, and that other challenges to NAGPRA might occur within each federal district court, as was the case with tests of the Antiquities Act in the ninth (*United States* v. *Diaz)* and tenth circuits (*United States* v. *Smyer*) of the U.S. Court of Appeals (Hutt, Jones, and McAllister 1992: 24–25) in the 1970s. The testing of NAGPRA has just begun, and both the scientific and American Indian communities are awaiting the results.

But the battle is not only being fought in the courts. A campaign, similar to one begun when NAGPRA was being proposed, has started. A nonprofit organization, Friends of America's Past, was formed in 1998. As stated on the organization's Internet site (www.friendsofpast.org), the group is "dedicated to promoting and advancing the rights of scientists and the public to learn about America's past." The goals are similar to those of the American Committee for the Preservation of Archaeological Collections (ACPAC), who fought to "prevent the anti-education, anti-museum, anti-archaeologist movement from destroying irreplaceable archaeological collections" (American Committee for the Preservation of Archaeological Collections 1990).

Again, the conflict in ownership and control of the past is evident. Does the "history" of the pre-Columbian inhabitants of the land now known as America belong to the current inhabitants, the dominant culture, or the descendants of the people who initially occupied that land?

In the previous chapters, varying degrees of American Indian control over archaeological and cultural resources have been described, with the control over the cultural resources of the United States hinging on the tribe's ability to organize efficiently. The Pawnee were able to influence not only state policy but also state archaeologists with the successful closure of the Indian Burial Pit of Salina, Kansas. The Colville were able to exert control over an archaeological site on private land and were able to influence both local and national archaeologists in a conflict revolving primarily around ethical, rather than scientific, issues. The Umatilla have brought the issue of control of ancient material into the court system.

But the Navajo make the most compelling case regarding the ability to organize effectively, to work within the system, and to control their own destiny—both past and future.

The repercussions of this control revolve primarily around the control of a cultural group over the amount and type of research carried out within that group's boundaries. For example, the 1992 amendments to the National Historic Preservation Act allow the Navajo Tribe to take over compliance duties for the act from the state historic preservation officers' offices for Arizona and New Mexico. It is *possible* (though not necessarily probable) that the Navajo Nation Historic Preservation Office could prevent archaeologists or anthropologists not totally sympathetic to the Navajo from conducting research on the Navajo Reservation by denying permits for cultural resources programs, by rejecting reports that were unflattering to the Navajo, or by preventing excavation of archaeological sites by denying excavation permits.

Through the passage of recent legislation (notably the NAGPRA and the 1992 amendments to the National Historic Preservation Act), American Indian groups have been given mechanisms for exerting control over the cultural resources within their tribal lands. It remains to be seen, however, whether those mechanisms will be utilized to exert such controls.

But the situation in America is not unique. The following chapter provides a glimpse into the situation facing indigenous populations in other industrialized countries.

10

⟋⟍ᴏ⟍ᴏ⋈ᴏ⟋ᴏ

Repatriation in a
Global Perspective

> The act of seeking reconciliation between archaeologists and in-
> digenous peoples sets up a process of consultation and interac-
> tion which tells us that this unknown post-colonial landscape will
> be created by us all, in a form as yet unknown. (Murray 1996:
> 219)

Archaeology's struggle to communicate with indigenous populations concerning the control of their cultural resources and
the repatriation of human remains is not limited to the United
States. Archaeologists were once accustomed to conducting archaeological research without considering the wishes of the indigenous population, but now these populations, generally "politically
weak, economically marginal, and culturally stigmatized members
of the national societies that have overtaken them and their lands"
(Dyck 1992: 1), are flexing their political muscles concerning the
protection of material cultural and the repatriation of human remains. As a result of this growth in ethnic and national identity, archaeologists must often negotiate a myriad of regulations and procedures.

This chapter offers a brief survey of the relationships between
indigenous populations and anthropologists in Canada, Australia,
New Zealand, and in Scandinavia.

CANADA

Relationships between First Nations of Canada and Canadian anthropologists are similar to that of American Indians and American anthropologists, and the practice of the disciplines on either side of the border share similar trajectories. A detailed analysis of these relationships will not be presented here; the reader is referred to *At a Crossroads: Archaeology and First Peoples in Canada* (1997). The volume, a collection of papers edited by George P. Nicholas and Thomas D. Andrews, offers a good view of the current status of archaeologist/First Nation relations in Canada.

In 1992, the Canadian Archaeological Association's (CAA) Committee on Archaeology and Aboriginal Heritage, cochaired by Bev Nicholson and Eldon Yellowhorn, began an examination of the relationships between professional archaeologists and aboriginal peoples.

Its mandate, as reported by Bev Nicholson, David Pokotylo, and Ron Williamson was

1. to develop, through extensive consultation with the aboriginal and archaeological communities, a draft statement of principles for ethical archaeological practice and minimum standards for intercommunity communication.
2. to examine policies and concepts to assist all levels of government (including aboriginal governments) to realize consensual management of aboriginal heritage features.
3. to encourage direct involvement of aboriginal people, through active recruitment programs, in professional archaeology. (1996: 4)

A draft set of guidelines was prepared and presented in an open forum at the CAA Annual Meeting in Edmonton in 1994; following the acceptance of comments from the membership, a revised Statement of Principles was prepared for recommendation of acceptance by the general membership at the 28th Annual CAA Conference in Kelowna in 1995. The final Statement of Principles for Ethical Conduct Pertaining to Aboriginal Peoples (Nicholson, Pokotylo, and Williamson 1996: 35) was passed at the 29th Annual Meeting of the CAA in Halifax by a vote of almost twenty-five to one (Rosenswig 1997: 99).

It is important to note that these guidelines deal with the relationship between archaeologists and aboriginal peoples, not to the overall practice of archaeology toward which the SAA Principles are oriented. Perhaps it is because of this orientation that the relationships between First Nations and anthropologists in Canada are relatively cordial.

The discovery of a human body in a glacier in August 1999 demonstrates some of the differences in the relations between natives and anthropologists in Canada and those of the United States.

Three people hunting sheep in a remote corner of British Columbia discovered the frozen remains of a human in a melting glacier in Wilderness Park in British Columbia on August 14, 1999, but the find was not reported until August 25.

Bill Hanlon, one of the hunters, described finding carved pieces of wood that "looked like a backpack. You could see the actual threading and the holes where it was sewn together" (quoted in Brooke 1999a). Also found were "a fur cloak, a broad-brimmed hat, a walking stick, a spear, and a leather pouch filled with fish and edible leaves" (Verrengia 1999).

The announcement of the find was delayed ten days so that archaeologists could consult with elders of the Champagne and Aishihik First Nations who, as part of a wider land claims settlement reached in 1995, maintain veto power over any archaeological work within the park as well as legal control over any artifacts discovered within the park.

But in sharp contrast to the situation between the Umatilla and American archaeologists over Kennewick, the elders favored obtaining scientific information from the find prior to its reburial. Ron Chambers, a tribal member of the park management board, is quoted as saying, "The elders did say that they felt it was as important to get as much information as possible from this person— that's kind of an endorsement of scientific study" (quoted in Brooke 1999a).

The framework for the study of the adult male called "Kwaday Dan Sinchi," the southern Tutchone words meaning "long-ago person found," was announced in September. Canadian government and tribal groups proposed to set up a scientific advisory panel to evaluate research proposals for scientific studies, and then turn the remains over to descendants for burial by the end of 2000 (Sorensen 1999a).

In spite of the agreement to allow the studies, Diane Strand, a heritage-resource officer for the Champagne and Aishihik First Nations, said the agreement was not unanimously endorsed: "You have one-third of the people saying 'Bury him,' one-third of the people saying 'You're doing the right thing,' and the other one-third saying 'We don't know.' But the goal is learning and educating" (quoted in Sorensen 1999a).

Eventually, radiocarbon tests performed on pieces of the hat and cloak found with the individual dated to sometime between A.D. 1415 and 1445 (Sorensen 1999b). Scientists are proposing further tests on the individual, including DNA tests to help determine cultural affiliation and paleobotanical studies of the plant materials found in the bag. The blood and tissues of the individual, if he truly died prior to the arrival of European explorers on the North American continent, might provide scientists with an understanding of some pathologies present in the aboriginal populations of the North America. Knut Fladmark, a British Columbian archaeologist, noted that the body could "throw light on nutrition, health standards, and perhaps diseases—which you don't have access to with bones" (quoted in Brooke 1999b).

Bob Charlie, chief of the Champagne and Aishihik First Nations, notes that the archaeologists have been respectful to the Nations' wishes: "Their willingness to cooperate has been quite pleasing to us. They have been very patient, because I'm sure they would have liked to jump ahead and plow ahead with it" (quoted in Brooke 1999b). Thus, archaeologists in this portion of Canada are cultivating a strong relationship with Canadian First Nations.

AUSTRALIA

Jane Hubert's analysis of the "reburial issue" in Australia provides a history of the relationships between Australian archaeologists and Australian Aboriginal populations, and outlines Aboriginal opposition to "the excavation of sacred sites, including burial sites, and the display and storage of Aboriginal skeletal remains in museums and university departments" (1994: 149). Additionally, John Mulvaney and Johan Kamminga's *Prehistory of Australia* (1999) offers a more recent examination of Australian prehistory and the relationships of archaeologists and Aboriginal populations.

Although the Commonwealth government assumed responsibility for Aboriginal affairs in 1967, administration was generally left to the separate states. The Archaeological and Aboriginal Relics Preservation Act 1972 (Victoria Act No. 8273/1972, since amended) was the first legislation aimed at protecting the heritage of Aboriginal people in Victoria. Later, the Aboriginal and Torres Strait Islander Heritage Protection Amendment Act of 1987 proclaimed "the Aboriginal people of Victoria are the rightful owners of their heritage and should be given responsibility for its future control and management" (quoted in Mulvaney 1991: 14). Basically, Australian federal law states that all pre-1770 remains are by definition Aboriginal and must be controlled by Aboriginal authorities (Jones and Harris 1999: 255). But who are the "Aboriginal people" of Australia?

In *The Australian Journal of Anthropology* Special Issue 2, "Reconsidering Aboriginality" (Thiele 1991a), a collection of authors provided a series of articles reflecting on the status of "Aboriginal Studies" in Australia. Jeff Archer (1991: 163) noted that "Aboriginality as a construction for purposes of political action has all the characteristic contradictions of nationalism," and Frank Lewins noted "it is not possible to keep Aboriginality and politics apart" (177). Steven Thiele argued Aboriginality involves "descentism," based "solely on the grounds of biological parentage" (1991b: 180). Alan Roughly wrote that race, nationality, possession, and difference were "the controlling and central terms in the written history of a racial discourse that must be continuously deconstructed" (211). Kenneth Maddock noted "The sacred site . . . enables possession (of the land) to be consummated" (231), while Lee Sackett detailed the stereotypical belief held by some that "aboriginal values and practices are somehow or another more 'ecologically sound' than those of non-Aborigines" (235). Finally, Iain Davidson noted that, in the changing relationships between archaeologists and Aborigines, "the motives of the Aboriginal and non-Aboriginal peoples in the cooperation have not always been the same" (256).

In 1984, the Australian Anthropological Association issued a policy supporting the reburial of post-1788 remains to communities (Meehan 1984) as well as the return of Aboriginal skeletal remains of known individuals, in the hopes of fostering a collaboration between indigenous populations and archaeologists. The policy also stressed that all other Aboriginal skeletal remains are of scientific importance and should not be destroyed through reburial or cremation (Jones and Harris 1999: 254).

But, in spite of the latter portion of the policy, the repatriation of Aboriginal human remains in a situation similar to that at Kennewick put a strain on Australian anthropologists. Human burials discovered by Alan Thorne in 1967 on the edge of Kow Swamp reservoir were excavated between 1968 and 1972. The salvage operation alongside an irrigation channel recovered approximately forty individuals who lived roughly 9,000 to 15,000 years ago. Cultural indicators included artifacts and pigment as grave goods and, although there was a variety of interment styles among the individuals, the availability of such a localized population of ancient humans caused anthropologists to view these remains as "a crucial statistical assemblage for any investigation of Aboriginal origins" (Mulvaney 1991: 14).

In August 1990, the Museum of Victoria presented the Kow Swamp Collection of human remains and associated grave goods to the Echuca Aboriginal Cooperative on the Murray River in central Victoria, a community that indicated it wished to accord those remains a mass reburial.

Mulvaney decried the reburial of the material, noting "the case merits record for its implications for intellectual freedom. . . . It is not simply the Kow Swamp relics which are at stake, but the future of past Aboriginal culture and the freedom of all peoples of any race to study it" (1991: 12). Since then, the Murray Black Collection that contained the remains of some individuals dating back 10,000 years has been returned for reburial (Mulvaney and Kamminga 1999: 9–10).

Like Mulvaney, Austin Gough was also concerned about any wholesale repatriation of human remains, writing:

> The humans whose remains have been excavated in the past seventy years were the predecessors of modern Aborigines, but not necessarily the direct ancestors of any particular Aboriginal group. . . . [I]t is absurd that one generation of activists . . . should claim the right to hide or destroy material that would be of immense value to future generations of Australians of all racial backgrounds. (1996: 133–34)

Another Australian anthropologist, Colin Pardoe, feels that scientists should not have the right to determine the ultimate disposition of human remains without the involvement of the indigenous population: "Some have distinguished between more recent remains which Aborigines may control and the older remains which belong to the world. This denies the concept of full and unfettered Aboriginal ownership of the past" (Pardoe 1992: 133). He goes on to say: "If I acknowledge Aboriginal ownership of their ancestor's bones, that is no different than asking permission to analyse [sic] bones from France, Italy, or wherever" (138).

NEW ZEALAND

Gareth D. Jones and Robyn J. Harris note that "Archeologists and anthropologists in New Zealand are facing the same ethical issues as have arisen in Australia, Britain, and the United States" (1998: 255). In 1990, the indigenous population of New Zealand, the Maori, was estimated to number approximately 435,000 (Morse 1997: 316). Maori landownership on New Zealand was first affected by the Treaty of Waitangi, signed February 6, 1840, whereby Maori chieftains agreed to be under the "government" of the Queen of England, and agreed to sell land to the Crown, while the Crown agreed to offer to the Maori "all the Rights and Privileges of British Subjects" (New Zealand 1840).

Abuses of the treaty continued until the Treaty of Waitangi Act in 1975, wherein the statute created "an independent and bicultural tribunal to receive complaints and hold hearings into alleged treaty violations" (Morse 1997: 318).

With the passage of the Resource Management Act of 1991, the relationship of Maori and their culture and traditions with their ancestral lands, water sites, and sacred sites was deemed to be of national importance. Thus, it became necessary to take Maori interests under consideration in the development of all regional land uses and in the review of major economic and other developmental projects likely to impact Maori environmental interests (Morse 1997: 319).

As anthropologists and historians become more involved in claims before the tribunals (formed under the Treaty of Waitangi Act), the ethics involved in doing research both for and on the Maori continue to be questioned.

E. T. Durie, in an article entitled "Ethics and Values" (1999), discusses ethical issues passed on to him by Waitangi Tribunal researchers that he feels need to be brought out for further discussion:

1. That only Maori should write on Maori matters.
2. That the opinions or recollections of kaumatua should not be subject to cross-examination or other challenge.
3. [When] groups who have commissioned researchers have sometimes required researchers to remove material unhelpful to the claimants' case or amend their conclusions, sometimes as a condition to being paid. Are there terms that researchers should negotiate with claimant groups beforehand?
4. Can a researcher commissioned by a tribal group publish the results of that research and even although the information is from public sources? What if the information relied as well, or exclusively, on private, oral opinions from within the tribe? Can a researcher who is not commissioned by a tribal group but who relies on information from tribal members, publish material without prior permission from them? What if the condition to publication is that certain conclusions be changed? Should the terms for giving information be settled beforehand?
5. Should evidence to the Waitangi Tribunal be publicly available? If it should be generally available, should parts be protected from use?
6. How far can researchers go with adverse comments on living people without prior consultation with them?
7. How widely should one consult with tribal persons?
8. If researchers rely entirely on public sources, are they still obliged to consult tribal members . . . [who] may wish to challenge the accuracy of those records and the opinions expressed?
9. Should scholars rely on given translations of Maori material or consult with local people for a better contextual interpretation? If the material is not translated should scholars use local interpreters? (1999: 11–14)

While supportive of a general code of ethics for researchers "as a guide and a shield from criticism" (Durie 1999: 13), he also notes how such a code might cause other problems. Citing the British

Columbia Supreme Court case *Delgamukw* v. *British Columbia*, an aboriginal title claim, he notes the court "rejected a large amount of anthropological evidence on the ground, amongst others, that the anthropologists were bound by a code of ethics that was too weighted to maintaining a current Indian view" (13).

These expanding Maori rights and involvement within the land management programs have also had direct influence on the practice of anthropology in New Zealand. As with other countries, repatriation issues are arising within New Zealand. The Maori are becoming increasingly active in determining the disposition of the skeletal remains and items of cultural significance (*taonga Maori*). Under current legislation, excavated material belongs to the Crown, and it cannot be excavated without a permit, the issuance of which is contingent on the approval of the local Maori community (Jones and Harris 1998: 255). Museums are also being chided to refrain from acting as the "final resting places for artefacts [sic] and to acknowledge the continuing relevance of *taonga* to a dynamic Maori culture and to New Zealand culture in general" (Hogan 1995).

As with other indigenous groups throughout the world, the Maori are calling for full responsibility for the control and management of their cultural heritage (Jones and Harris 1998: 255). Since each individual *iwi* (roughly "tribe") is responsible for guidelines relating to the appropriate treatment of archaeological remains, there is no nationwide policy concerning the disposition of ancestral Maori human remains (*koiwi tangata*) or cultural materials.

Karl Gilles and Gerard O'Regan (1994) discuss the policy of one of the larger tribal groups of New Zealand. The Murihiku resolution of *koiwi tangata* management specifies that the *iwi* retains authority and control over ancestral bones, and that their collection and possession by anyone other than the tribe itself as abhorrent and culturally insensitive. It notes a clear preference that the remains be left *in situ* where possible, and undisturbed. For those remains already disturbed, it requests repatriation to the *iwi*, but also recognizes that scientific investigation can play a role in understanding tribal ancestry. The tribe does, however, reserve the right to edit for reasons of cultural sensitivity any material proposed for publication (Jones and Harris 1998: 255).

If, as Gordan Pullar notes, "Western scientists see time as linear . . . [and] indigenous people . . . circular" (1994: 19), then time to the

Maori differs in a significant direction from either perspective. For the Western viewpoint, the past lies behind and the future is spread in front of the person, but to the Maori culture, the past is in front because events in the past are well known and the future is behind because it cannot be seen and is unknowable (Jones and Harris 1998: 256).

As has been outlined in this short discussion of the situation in New Zealand anthropology, local Maori community involvement with the permitting processes required before cultural material can be excavated is increasing. The Maori are also exerting more control over the way that museums handle cultural materials, and are trying to develop "keeping places" where important cultural material may be kept for the benefit of the Maori without necessitating an actual transfer of material. This increased control will lead to more involvement with archaeologists and anthropologists and will result in the Maori having a greater voice in the development of their prehistories and histories.

SCANDINAVIA

The Sami are an indigenous peoples who live in four separate countries—Finland, Norway, Sweden, and Russia. Formerly called "Lapplanders" by others, in 1990, the population estimates were 17,000 in Sweden, 5,700 in Finland, and over 30,000 in Norway (Morse 1997: 310). No current figures are available for the Sami population of Russia.

The Sami are thought to have originated somewhere in what is now northeastern Russia, although there does remain some points of contention (Olsson and Lewis 1995: 148). Increased movement into the area began following contact with the Vikings in the eighth or ninth century, and the Sami were forced from their more favored area further northward. Sven E. Olsson and Dave Lewis (1995: 249) note that the efforts by Denmark and Sweden to control the Sami resulted in three major responses: the emergence of a coastal Sami culture based mainly on fishing and supplemented by agriculture; the emergence of an inland-Sami culture where agriculture was supplemented by hunting, fishing, and some reindeer herding; and a nomadic Sami culture drawn from both the coastal and inland-

Sami groups mainly occupied with taming, tending, and herding reindeer.

Marjut Aikio and Pekka Aikio document the paucity of Sami archaeology and the desire by some Sami archaeology students in Norway to halt archaeological excavations until "the Sami archaeologists themselves can take over and perform this invaluable work" (1994: 128). And, as part of an attempt to involve the Sami of Sweden more in the process, a new Program of Sami Studies has been set up under the Department of Archaeology at the University of Umea, which encourages the Sami to develop a new curriculum and graduate program integrating theory, method, and practice in archaeology using a Sami cultural perspective.

Inga-Maria Mulk notes that traces of Sami cultures usually are "hunting pits, hearths, hut foundations, graves, and sacrificial places" (1997: 123), with a great number of these sacrificial places investigated by various authors. With the intensification of church missionizing in the seventeenth century came the persecution of Sami shamans (*noaiddit*), who were forced to turn over their drums, which were destroyed by being set on fire (130).

Some have been able to identify Sami places based on old tax records. For example, Israel Ruong discusses how the villages of Tingiwara and Siggewara can be located by identifying the marshes taxed by the Crown and that the old Sami names of the villages of Jokkmokk and Arvidsjaur indicate that their winter villages later became court seats and church villages when the Swedish sovereignty was established in Sami territory (1982: 25).

Perhaps because there have been few archaeological excavations on Sami cultural sites, requests for repatriation have not progressed rapidly in the Sami territories. If Mulk is true in her belief that "to this very day there are Sami who have a knowledge of old Sami popular beliefs, some of them practicing as medicine-men" (1997: 130), the repatriation of such cultural items as shaman drums within museum collections looms on the horizon.

CONCLUSIONS

With the growth of ethnic and nationalistic awareness, archaeologists are being forced to reexamine the relationship between the treatment of the cultural materials and human remains of indigenous populations and that of the dominant societies. Such examination, while perhaps disconcerting to the individual archaeologist, strengthens the discipline by allowing the development of alternative means of viewing the past.

The variety of programs among indigenous populations trying to regain control of their cultural heritage is mirrored among American Indian tribes. The interruption of land tenure, the suppression of native language, the view of the native as an inferior race, and the marginalization of the group as a whole is not only descriptive of the situation as it has occurred in the United States, but is a common thread in the history of the colonization of indigenous nations throughout the world.

While the survey has taken only a brief look at the situation in other countries, inherent in the study of the relationship between indigenous populations and archaeologists is the idea of "standing." Lawrence Rosen questioned: "Who has the right to excavate, or prevent the excavation of, a recent or ancient burial site, and on what authority is that right to be based?" (1980: 6). While recent burials may be protected under the common law of a dominant government, the same law may be mute regarding the protection of ancient burials. Also, the scientific view of a burial as a resource for gaining information about the culture that interred the individual is often at odds with the religious view of a burial as the final resting place of an individual that must be protected from disturbance.

Most repatriation and burial protection laws are requiring the involvement of indigenous populations in the decision-making processes now more than ever, but the conflict between the wishes of those populations and the scientific community still remains. The discipline of archaeology is struggling to balance the wishes of indigenous individuals (American Indian, Canadian First Nations, Australian Aborigine, Maori, or Sami) concerning the ultimate disposition of an object with the desires of scientists.

In the United States, Clement Meighan, a vocal opponent of reburial and repatriation, argued that "the belief that archaeology belongs to Indians removes it from the heritage of all of the citizens" (1992: 707) and that laws "which ignore time and assume that everything, regardless of age, is directly related to living people, are not scientifically valid" (709). Additionally, the court case brought by the six anthropologists against the Corps of Engineers in the Kennewick situation is a further attempt to legally identify the rights of indigenous populations over extremely old material.

Much like Meighan in America, Mulvaney in Australia feels that, while Australian "archaeologists support the return of remains from recent generations to local communities for reburial, because social and spiritual considerations outweigh other factors," for older remains, "their kin cannot be presumed to have shared the same cultural values or religious concepts of this generation" (1991: 16). Pardoe notes "Aboriginal demands for ownership and control of their heritage has been consistent for over a decade" (1992: 133), but he also notes the conflict between archaeologists and Aborigines increases when "Pleistocene remains (over 10,000 years old) have been slated for reburial" (133).

And so the question remains: To whom does the past belong? Do the descendants of the founding population have the right to control access to the evidence of their culture, or should that access be open to anyone, including those who have spent their lives focused on learning about all of humanity? While it might be reasonable to believe that an indigenous group should have the right to determine the fate of their direct ancestors, many people question their right to have control over cultural material that may be equally related to an entire population.

This chapter is not meant to provide an in-depth analysis of the state of affairs between indigenous populations and archaeologists throughout the world, but rather to illustrate the variation and similarities in the development of programs undertaken by indigenous populations to take control of certain aspects of their past.

Many of the situations that archaeologists in North America face are being encountered by archaeologists in Australia and New Zealand, and many of the concerns expressed by the Sami in the Scandinavian countries have been expressed by First Nations in Canada and American Indian tribes in the United States.

It is imperative that archaeologists examine their relationships with indigenous populations with whom they work, and that they strengthen them if they wish to continue working with the cultural remains of first nations throughout the world. These relationships must become symbiotic, rather than parasitic, and they must be based on the wishes and needs of the indigenous population rather than solely on the wishes and needs of the archaeologist.

11

꩜

Indigenous Archaeology

In the previous ten chapters, I have tried to draw attention to certain aspects of the relationship between American Indians and American archaeology, as well as offering a glimpse of the discipline's relationship with indigenous populations in other parts of the world. I have presented some facets within the fields of ethics and historic preservation legislation that I feel control the majority of archaeologists' relations with American Indians here in the United States.

I also have tried to show that American Indians do not have any singular way of dealing with archaeology and archaeologists, but rather have adopted various processes to suit their particular situations. It has been more than ten years since *Preservation on the Reservation: Native Americans, Native American Lands and Archaeology* (Klesert and Downer 1990) presented in-depth and sometimes pointed discussions by tribal groups and archaeologists about the state of the discipline at that time, and it seems time for another such conference.

I have enjoyed updating the manuscript from the time when research for the dissertation left off, and have particularly enjoyed reading the stacks of newspaper articles and surfing Internet sites for new and exciting revelations about Kennewick Man/Patrick Stewart, and I have even enjoyed following the debate in academic publications concerning the implications of so old an ancestor.

I have done all that in this manuscript and am trying to finish up, but what do I do now?

FEED THE HUNGRY, CLOTHE THE POOR, AND ESTABLISH GLOBAL PEACE

Okay, perhaps the heading for this section is a rather tall order, but sometimes I feel that is what final chapters are supposed to be. This is the point where, having invested a great deal of your time in the reading, analyzing, and digestion of the data, you are expecting dessert. But there really is no dessert, only comments, suggestions, and questions. And, even before I get started, I want to state that I speak only from the viewpoint of one archaeologist who has worked with (and happens to be) American Indians.

There is a common thread that runs through this book—the conflict that exists between indigenous populations and archaeologists throughout the world. In my opinion, there are two main points around which this conflict is based: the perceived threat to the human remains and funerary objects of an indigenous population by a dominant, industrialized society, and the wish of the indigenous population to gain control over the construction of their culture-history (occasionally even through a deconstruction of that history). In my opinion, all other problems spring from one or both of these two wellheads.

In my early years of archaeology, I ascribed to the view that, if we archaeologists only were able to teach American Indians, they would understand the importance of what we do. I recall when, at the end of a presentation I made at the University of California at Los Angeles in 1978, a young American Indian woman asked me, "Do you have to be an atheist to be an archaeologist?" I did not ask her what she meant, because I knew immediately what she was talking about. I did not answer with a discussion of the amount of information that graves hold to bioarchaeologists, or the benefits of archaeology from a global perspective, but rather with another question: "If graves must be dug, would you rather them be dug by someone who respected them or someone who didn't care?" Neither one of us really got an answer that day.

The teacher-student relationship requires that one person have greater power than the other, something that American Indians continue to fight against. As both American Indians and archaeologists must realize, it is more important to learn than to teach.

It is unclear whether a program of mutual education would produce major changes in the attitudes of archaeologists or American Indians. It is unlikely that there are many individuals who have not heard of, been involved in, or have an opinion on the conflict at one level or another, and also unlikely that the individuals who might be swayed to either side of the argument would have major impacts on the conflict.

On a project-specific basis, education is necessary. The archaeologist must educate affected cultural groups about a project so that they can have an informed understanding of the reasons for the project, the types of information being sought, and the implications and utility of the study to the group studied and to archaeology. This inability to communicate effectively has been one of the discipline's major failures.

Cultural groups should also be involved in educating the anthropologist about their wishes concerning information that may be present, the ways they may want to involve themselves in the project, the types of information they desire obtaining, and any restrictions they feel might be necessary for the protection of information they feel should not be released to the general public. Such mutual education, on a project-by-project or one-to-one basis, provides both parties with an understanding of what would be expected of both groups should such programs be undertaken. This level of education should already be built into the consultation requirements set forth in federal legislation.

In examining the struggle between archaeologists and American Indians, Randall H. McGuire notes it is "not just a problem of public relations or of education" (1992a: 828). He recognizes the need for a dialogue between American Indians and archaeologists, a dialogue that he says will "fundamentally alter the practice of archeology in the United States . . . , our perceptions of the past, how we deal with living Native Americans, how we train our students, and how we present our results to each other and the general public" (828).

He goes on to assert that archaeology is the study of people, not things, that those people have a present and a future, as well as a past, and that the archaeologists must integrate the concerns of the American Indian people with their research. The same must be said of all indigenous populations throughout the world.

Archaeologists must become aware that they are not the only source of protection for cultural resources. Historically, archaeologists have been the primary agents for protecting cultural resources, although, at the same time, they may also have been the primary agents in their destruction. The problem arises when "protection" or "destruction" remain undefined. Their definitions are often culturally determined and based in cultural backgrounds that see results differently. For example, to archaeologists, protection means preventing the destruction of the archaeological site due to pot hunting or construction activities, while to some American Indian groups, protection also means the prevention of scientific excavations.

However, American Indian groups and archaeologists share a desire to protect the cultural heritage (regardless of whose it is) from *unnecessary* or unwarranted destruction from all sources, as well as the protection of cultural material from effects arising from the quest for commercial gain. This shared desire should be utilized to the maximum extent possible if gains are to be made.

Archaeologists are also trying to understand and develop the steps that can be taken to help prevent potential conflicts before they happen rather than after the fact. I, K. Anne Pyburn, and Pam Cressey offer suggestions to practicing archaeologists to allow them to be able to work more effectively with local and/or descendant communities:

1. Identify the community with which they will be involved.
2. Form partnerships beyond archaeology.
3. Understand the legal boundaries involved in the process.
4. Communicate effectively.
5. Recognize diverse decision-making structures.
6. Place the goals of the project ahead of personal and private goals.
7. Be aware of social and gender issues. (2000: 73–81)

Proper training in these seven areas would ensure that archaeologists and the affected group have a strong possibility for success. Some anthropologists might wish to expand the list to include various subsets of the population or perhaps emphasize one of the seven over the others, but the inclusion of all in a consistently applied program would maintain public involvement in cultural resources management.

Federal laws that now serve to regulate the protection of cultural resources form the backbone of what I perceive to be legislated ethics ("legislethics"). The Antiquities Act of 1906, the National Historic Preservation Act of 1966, the National Environmental Policy Act of 1969, Executive Order 11593 in 1971, and the Archaeological and Historic Preservation Act of 1974 have gone beyond the establishment of broad guidelines and more into those portions of compliance archaeology that were once left to the judgment of individual archaeologists.

The American Indian Religious Freedom Act (AIRFA) of 1978 *required* consultation with affected Indian groups when projects might impact sacred areas. The Archaeological Resources Protection Act (ARPA) of 1979 also required consultation with the "affected tribe," but additionally allowed American Indian groups to attach terms and conditions to archaeological permits issued under this law for excavations on tribal lands. It also required "consideration" of the spirit of AIRFA. The final rules and regulations also required federal land managers to identify Indian tribes with aboriginal or historical ties to lands under the manager's control and to gather information on the location of sacred or religious locations. Ultimately, AIRFA and ARPA forced archaeologists to establish lines of communication (consultation) with the Indian tribes affected by archaeological projects and to respect tribal wishes, at least if those wishes were made a part of an antiquities permit.

Repatriation legislation such as the National Museum of the American Indian Act and the Native American Graves Protection and Repatriation Act (NAGPRA) developed procedures for returning archaeological, cultural, and skeletal material to American Indian groups when cultural affinity could be proven, and expanded the definition of "Indian lands" to include all lands (public and private) within the external boundaries of a reservation.

These last laws have made a considerable impact on choices once left to the individual: they required consultation with American Indian groups, introduced more restrictive federal legislation and procedures, gave congressional recognition to control (through permitting procedures and through right of ownership) to American Indian groups over cultural material on federal lands that were once their homeland and to lands that may come under federal control, and they focused the process of consultation by determining which American Indian groups should be contacted by the archaeologist.

The impacts of these regulations on the "ethics" of archaeologists focused on consultation and communication. The archaeologist has been "forced" to consult with, and often accede to, the wishes of American Indian groups that control the lands on which the desired research was to take place. Decisions regarding the excavation of human remains have also been affected with the passage of NAGPRA.

Archaeologists who responded to my research questionnaire showed a tendency to side with the owner of the property that held the archaeological site, while at the same time weighing the concerns of the parties involved. The research also showed this tendency to be one that was affected by experience, education, and age.

"Younger" or "newer" archaeologists tended to respond that they felt landownership should play a strong or moderate role in excavation decisions, while older archaeologists tended to respond that they felt landownership should play only a minor role in decisions to excavate. This may relate to the impact of legislative control of permitting procedures based on land status or to the time period when the responder began his or her training, or it may indicate that older archaeologists view cultural resources, regardless of the status of the land on which they rest, as the cultural patrimony of all people of the United States, and not the cultural patrimony of the descendants of those who produced them.

Continued legislative treatment of the problem will force archaeologists to reexamine their stances, resign themselves to the situation, align themselves with groups or factions that are most supportive of their views, or actively lobby for the enactment or amendment of legislation more in line with their views. As John C. Ravesloot, the cultural resources coordinator for the Gila River Indian Community, notes: "Archaeologists can either accept the fact that American archaeology is changing . . . or bury their heads in their federal regulations and/or academic ivory towers. If avoidance behavior is the path selected, we can be assured that new federal statutes will be introduced to force archaeologists to change business as usual" (1997: 173–74).

And what about American Indians and their relationships with American archaeology?

The case studies in this book serve as examples of the various levels of development within tribal cultural resource programs in the United States. Looking back, the reader should be aware of some of the commonalties they exhibit and the problems they illustrate.

The Navajo Nation, by most accounts, has one of the most active and far-reaching archaeology programs in the United States. It not only conducts archaeological surveys on the reservation, but it also consults actively with Navajo elders to gain additional information and understanding on the types of impacts that archaeological programs might have on the local population. As such, and in conjunction with the Hopi Cultural Resources Program and the Zuni Archaeological Program, it provides an unchallenged opportunity for a regional archaeology with a "native perspective" in the United States.

However, as both Richard M. Begay (1997) and Rena Martin (1997) acknowledge, traditional people of the Navajo Nation still have a problem with the disturbance of archaeological sites by archaeologists, even those employed to help the nation. The fact that the Navajo Nation must comply with federal regulations that impose a foreign preservation system on them makes the development of a truly "Navajo" preservation system, absent a change in federal regulations, nearly impossible.

The Pawnee situation in Kansas illustrates not only what can be accomplished when American Indians and archaeologists work toward a common goal, but also the problems when institutions get caught up in the *ownership* of objects rather than the *stewardship* of them. The insensitivity of the exhibition of human remains at the Salina Burial Pit was felt by all involved, and the resultant closure of the tourist trap was beneficial to all parties, but the politicization of the Pawnee quest for the reburial and repatriation of human remains and grave goods held by the Nebraska State Historical Society serves as an important reminder that not everything we work for comes easy, and, if we choose to ignore each other, we all suffer.

The situation at East Wenatchee is indicative of what might arise as a result of inadequate communication. The tribal groups involved (the Colville and Yakama) were amenable to the first excavations at the East Wenatchee Clovis Cache, primarily because the testing was carried out by a local archaeologist with good relations with the tribal groups. But once further excavations were proposed by an "outside" archaeologist who had not developed good communication pathways with local tribal groups, and once the "possibility" arose (no matter how remote) that human remains might be found, the tribes utilized public opinion to reinforce their viewpoint.

Ultimately, the tribes were able to prevent the completion of the proposed excavation and to influence the regional archaeological society to protect the archaeological site and the cultural material. Perhaps the most important result of the situation was that the tribes were able to exert influence over the disposition of cultural materials nearly 10,000 years old that came from private property.

The Kennewick situation, far from over, is perhaps the most intricately interwoven example of those presented here. Resulting from miscommunication (between the archaeologists, officials, government agencies, and tribal groups involved), and the misapplication or misinterpretation of legislation (NAGPRA and ARPA), Kennewick nonetheless is performing a needed function.

The court challenge that the anthropologists have filed will serve to further identify the shortcomings of NAGPRA, but, perhaps more importantly, it will identify the extent that the dominant culture can "appropriate" the history of an indigenous population in the name of knowledge. While not truly a conflict between science and religion, as some have portrayed it, it is, nonetheless, a conflict of philosophical traditions.

TOWARD AN INDIGENOUS ARCHAEOLOGY

The discipline of archaeology has undergone a dramatic change over the last thirty years in relation to the wishes of indigenous populations, and even more so within the last ten. Even though there have always been some archaeologists attuned to the wishes of descendant populations, it was the passage of repatriation legislation during the last decade of the century that led to a more widespread involvement of indigenous populations with American archaeology.

While the development of a truly indigenous archaeology will never happen until indigenous populations control the quality and quantity of archaeology performed within their homelands, there have been steps taken to help the discipline move in that direction. Individual archaeologists have become more aware of the inequities between parties involved in the relationship and of the inherent conflict involved in the archaeologists' concept of a "collective past." Alice Beck Kehoe, in discussing this "collective past," notes that archaeologists might have again presupposed that American Indians want to "share" their past (1998: 215). According to Larry Zimmerman (1995), archaeologists talk about sharing the past and sharing history when in reality they want a convenient means of maintaining an upper hand. He writes: "The problem is control. I sense that . . . most archaeologists would be reluctant to relinquish control" (66).

So, then, where does archaeology's future lie?

The hope for an indigenous archaeology rests on groups who know how to use the system to get the results they want as well as on those who will push to modify that system to better fit the beliefs of indigenous people. By determining the path of the programs that study the early populations of their area, indigenous populations can influence not only the outcomes of those programs but also the extent and quality of knowledge obtained. Through their influence, the discipline can rise beyond the image it currently carries as an esoteric discipline producing data of benefit to no one other than archaeologists.

The development of an indigenous archaeology must also extend beyond the mere establishment of tribal cultural resource management programs where nontribal people are responsible for the day-to-day management of the archaeological resources of the tribe. Though it is important for a tribe to control the archaeology that is conducted on their lands (both on existing reservations and traditional homelands) and to be actively involved in the process of consultation on those projects that impact their resources, it is more important that tribal individuals become archaeologists qualified to lead and manage archaeological projects and to influence the development of interpretations about their resources.

Two non-Indian archaeologists, Kurt E. Dongoske and Roger Anyon (1997), write about their relationships with the tribal groups

for which they work (or did work). They note the conflict they often encounter between their role as tribal cultural resource managers, as professional archaeologists, and as advocates for tribal positions with which they might sometimes disagree. They also note
the reality that "many agencies apply an ethnocentric approach to
the management of historic properties that favors western values
over Native American values" (195).

   I do not see a truly indigenous archaeology developing until there
is a major change in the way that archaeology views ownership and
protection. Only when indigenous groups are able to control not
only the physical manifestations of their culture but also what
should be protected and how "protection" is defined will indigenous archaeology flourish.

PARIAH OR PIRANHA?

As I close this chapter, I feel it important that the reader understand
the difficulty indigenous people encounter when they choose archaeology as a career. Many American Indians cannot understand
why an American Indian would participate in a discipline that has
made its living off of the bones and artifacts of ancestors, and often consider that individual either a social outcast (pariah) or a carnivore, feeding off human flesh (piranha).

   Perhaps archaeologists have justly earned the feelings that American Indians have for them. They are, by and large, often thick-
skinned individuals wrapped up in the past with an inadequate
understanding of the way their work influences the present and the
descendants of those whose past they study. Archaeologists are
slow to change, but they are changing.

   I agree that archaeologists have the training to offer the "scientific" side of the story held by the past, and I also agree that such
viewpoints need to be illustrated, but archaeologists are rather hesitant to accept that there might be other sides of that story, which
are equally valid, and that American Indians do not have the same
power to present their sides of the story.

   I spoke with an American Indian friend who disputed this statement in a rather interesting way. In reading my article concerning
public policy and American Indian concerns (Watkins 2000), he said

he felt I was wrong when I said American Indians do not have a voice in the discipline. He told me that he felt that American Indians do have a voice, and that they should exercise that voice to be certain that archaeologists have the data to back up American Indian claims for relationships with ancient populations: "You have to have the DNA and craniometric and osteological data, they [the archaeologists] tell me, in order to make those claims [for relationships with ancient populations], and I tell them they should, by God, go out and get that data!"

Basically he was saying that American Indians, rather than lamenting the fact that archaeology has little to offer that is relevant to them, should actively push archaeologists to develop research questions and programs that benefit the tribes, and also to use archaeology itself to provide solid evidence to back up any counterclaims they present.

For those of us caught in the middle, the study of the past is often exciting and confusing, dangerous and delightful. We do sometimes feel, as Navajo anthropology student Davina TwoBears notes, "as though a Native American is not even a person or human, but a very complex, interesting thing" (2000: 16).

But our roles in both worlds are continually being revised. We are asked to provide technical assistance to tribal groups about specific archaeological or compliance issues, but are reviled and distrusted for being archaeologists. We are forced to sit through numerous recitations of the ills inflicted on American Indians by past legions of anthropologists and federal officials before we are given the opportunity to present our most recent explanation of federal regulations. And we are called "Camp Indians" if we explain the federal regulations in an honest manner if it is not the one the tribes want to hear. It is more difficult to be liked when one "tells it like it is" than when one glosses over issues and placates the public.

Throughout my thirty-plus years in archaeology, I have seen the discipline become aware of American Indian concerns about the control of archaeological sites and cultural materials of the United States. I followed the protests of more radical American Indians who were committed to making the public aware of the need to change that control to a more evenhanded approach to studying the past, and have worked within the system to try to offer an American Indian voice in marble halls.

I worked within the federal government to try to get American Indian concerns with federal archaeology known, and, although I might not have made any drastic changes, I like to think I might have at least helped lead the way toward the changes that took place in the 1990s. I still work within the system to try to get American Indian concerns at least heard on a national level.

I have found myself caught up in the question of not only what the future holds for me but also my place in the past. Given the opportunity to start over, would I still become an archaeologist? I can easily answer "yes," with only a moment's hesitation. The past is more alive for me now than it ever has been, and the future more bright. The possibilities of truly understanding humanity's role in the natural world is so much more available now than ever before, as is the information on the methods and manners by which humans finally colonized this patch of land called the "New World" by "Old World" explorers.

But we are in the midst of a war over the heritage of that world. Archaeologists and American Indians are battling over the physical and spiritual control of one of America's earliest inhabitants. Would the reburial of "The Ancient One" tomorrow destroy that information? It might make a portion of it less available, but the information is there, in other places, waiting to be found. Perhaps this is one of those battles that archaeologists need to reexamine. What is at stake? Is it the freedom of Western science to continue to operate as it has in the past, as a self-appointed guardian of a self-defined truth, or is it the opportunity to develop a more meaningful blend between Western science and non-Western beliefs concerning the philosophy of the past?

I believe in the utility of archaeology, not as an esoteric science that neatly sorts pot shards and arrowheads into even rows, but as a collection of methods and theories that offer us insights into the ways that people in the past coped with their daily lives, their environments, their questions, and their uncertainties. Perhaps, archaeologists have forgotten that those were real people, with hopes, fears, pains, and joys. I know American Indians do not forget that those beings were human, whether they knew them or not.

That is what archaeology needs more than ever, a spirit of humanity, a driving desire to find out about the personality of the past. That is what indigenous archaeology can bring to the discipline, a viewpoint that refuses to be "objective" and embraces the emotional, one that pursues not "truth" but understanding, and one that includes all facets of what it is to be human on the brink of an exciting adventure.

Bibliography

Adams, E. Charles
1984 Archeology and the Native American: A Case at Hopi. In *Ethics and Values in Archeology*. Edited by E. Green, 236–42. The Free Press, London.

Aikens, C. Melvin
1990 Recent Developments in the Colville Confederated Tribes' Cultural Resources Management Program. In *Preservation on the Reservation: Native Americans, Native American Lands and Archaeology*. Edited by A. Klesert and A. Downer, 301–6. Navajo Nation Papers in Anthropology Number 26. Navajo Nation Archaeology Department and the Navajo Nation Historic Preservation Department, Windowrock.

Aikio, Marjut, and Pekka Aikio
1994 A Chapter in the History of the Colonization of Sami Lands: The Forced Migration of Norwegian Reindeer Sami to Finland in the 1800s. In *Conflict in the Archaeology of Living Traditions*. Edited by R. Layton, 116–30. Routledge, New York.

Alexander, Cheryl, and Henry Becker
1978 The Use of Vignettes in Survey Research. *Public Opinion Quarterly* 42(1):93–104.

American Anthropological Association
1971 Principles of Professional Responsibility (with Amendments).

Reprinted in *Ethics and Values in Archeology.* Edited by E. Green, 29–35. The Free Press, London.

1990 Revised Principles of Professional Responsibility. Reprinted in *Ethics and the Profession of Anthropology: Dialogue for a New Era,* appendix 1. Edited by C. Fluehr-Lobban, 274–79. University of Pennsylvania Press, Philadelphia.

1991a Reburial Commission Report. *Anthropology Newsletter* 32(3), March.

1991b Smithsonian Sets New Policy on Indian Remains. *Anthropology Newsletter* 32(4), April.

1998 Code of Ethics of the American Anthropological Association. *Anthropology Newsletter* 39(6).

American Committee for the Preservation of Archaeological Collections
1990 *ACPAC Newsletter.* September. Whittier, California.

Anderson, Christopher
1990 Repatriation of Cultural Property: A Social Process. *Museum* #165, 42(1):54–55.

Anderson, Duane
1985 Reburial: Is It Reasonable? *Archaeology* 38(5):48–51.

Andrus, Cecil D., Chairman
1979 *American Indian Religious Freedom Act Report, P.L. 95-341.* Federal Agencies Task Force.

Anonymous
1970 Indian Skeleton. *Akwesasne Notes* 2(6):12. Rooseveltown, New York.

1971 Don't Exploit Our Dead or Our Ceremonies or Our Dances. *Akwesasne Notes* 3(6):1. Rooseveltown, New York.

1990a Free at Last: Spirits of Plains Indians Can Rest after Reburial. *Wichita Eagle,* 7 April.

1990b History, Controversy Both Buried at Clovis Site. *Spokane Chronicle,* 3 December.

Anyon, Roger
1991 Protecting the Past, Protecting the Present: Cultural Resources and American Indians. In *Protecting the Past.* Edited by G. S. Smith and J. E. Ehrenhard, 215–22. CRC Press, Boca Raton, Florida.

Anyon, Roger, and T. J. Ferguson
1995 Cultural Resources Management at the Pueblo of Zuni, New Mexico. *Antiquity* 69:919–30.

Archer, Jeff
1991 Ambiguity in Political Ideology: Aboriginality as Nationalism. In Reconsidering Aboriginality. *Australian Journal of Anthropology*, Special Issue 2. Edited by S. Thiele, 161–69. Anthropological Society of New South Wales, Sydney.

Associated Press
1990a Kansas Buys Indian Burial Pit to Rebury Skeletons. *Kansas City Times*, 5 January.

1990b Artifact Dig Ends, But Not Controversy. *Spokane Chronicle*, 28 November.

Attwood, Bain, and John Arnold (editors)
1992 *Power, Knowledge, and Aborigines*. La Trobe University Press, Bundoora, Victoria.

Begay, Daryl R.
1991 Navajo Preservation: The Success of the Navajo Nation Historic Preservation Department. *CRM* 14(4):1, 4.

Begay, Richard M.
1997 "The Role of Archaeology on Indian Lands: The Navajo Nation." In *Native Americans and Archaeologists: Stepping Stones to Common Ground*. Edited by N. Swidler, K. Dongoske, R. Anyon, and A. Downer, 161–66. AltaMira Press, Walnut Creek, California.

Begley, Sharon, and Andrew Murr
1999 The First Americans. *Newsweek*, 26 April, 50–57.

Belson, William A.
1981 *The Design and Understanding of Survey Questions*. Gower Publishing Co., Ltd. Aldershot, England.

Benallie, Larry, Jr.
1997 Archaeology and Ethnography on the Navajo Nation and Management of the Cultural Landscape. Paper presented at the 51st National Preservation Conference, National Trust for Historic Preservation, Santa Fe.

Benedict, Ruth R.
1946 *The Chrysanthemum and the Sword*. Houghton Mifflin Press, Boston.

Berenson, Mark L., David M. Levine, and David Rindskopf
1988 *Applied Statistics: A First Course*. Prentice Hall, Englewood Cliffs, New Jersey.

Bettinger, Robert
1991 *Hunter-gatherers: Archaeological and Evolutionary Theory*. Plenum Press, New York.

Biolsi, Thomas, and Larry Zimmerman (editors)
1997 *Indians and Anthropologists: Vine Deloria Jr., and the Critique of Anthropology*. University of Arizona Press, Tucson.

Blair, Bowen
1979 Indian Rights: Native Americans versus American Museums—A Battle for Artifacts. *American Indian Law Review* 7(1):125–54.

Bradford, Kim
1998 Hearing Set to Discuss Handling of Old Bones. *Tri-City Herald*, May 16. Electronic version at http://www.kennewick-man.com/news/051698.html. Last accessed: July 27, 2000.

Brooke, James
1999a Ancient Man Uncovered in Canadian Ice: Hunter Preserved with Clothing, Tools. *San Francisco Chronicle*, 25 August, 1.

1999b Lost Worlds Rediscovered as Canadian Glaciers Melt. *New York Times*, 5 October. Electronic version at http://www.nytimes.com/library/national/science/archeology-index.html, Keyword = Sinchi. Last accessed: July 27, 2000.

Brugge, David M.
1983 Navajo Prehistory and History to 1850. In *Southwest*. Edited by A. Ortiz, 489–501. Handbook of North American Indians, vol. 10. Smithsonian Institution Press, Washington, D.C.

1986 *Tsegai: An Archaeological Ethnohistory of the Chaco Region*. U.S. Department of the Interior, National Park Service, Washington, D.C.

Buikstra, Jane
1981 A Specialist in Cemetery Studies Looks at the Reburial Issue. *Early Man* 3:26–27.

Champe, J. L. et al.
1961 Four Statements for Archaeology. *American Antiquity* 27:137–39.

Coleman, Michael
1998 Tribes Want Remains Reburied. *Albuquerque Journal*, 11 December.

Columbia Broadcasting System
1998 Kennewick Man, Leslie Stahl, producer. *Sixty Minutes.*

Cummings, Calvin R.
1988 A Matter of Ethics . . . SOPA *Newsletter* 12(2):1–3.

Davidson, Iain
1991 Archaeologists and Aborigines. In Reconsidering Aboriginality. *Australian Journal of Anthropology*, Special Issue 2. Edited by S. Thiele, 247–58. Anthropological Society of New South Wales, Sydney.

Davis, Hester A.
1984 Approaches to Ethical Problems by Archaeological Organizations. In *Ethics and Values in Archeology*. Edited by E. Green, 13–21. The Free Press, London.

Del Bene, Terry, and Kimball Banks
1990 Skeletons in the Closet: An Assessment of North Dakota's Procedures for Protecting Human Remains. Paper presented at the 48th Annual Meeting of the Plains Anthropological Society, Oklahoma City.

Deloria, Vine, Jr.
1969 *Custer Died for Your Sins: An Indian Manifesto*. The Macmillan Company, London.

De Maio, Theresa J. (editor)
1983 *Approaches to Developing Questionnaires*. Statistical Policy Working Paper 10, Statistical Policy Office, Office of Information and Regulatory Affairs, Office of Management and Budget, Washington, D.C.

Dincauze, Dena
1985 Report on the Conference on Reburial Issues. *Bulletin of the Society for American Archaeology* 3(5):1–3.

Dongoske, Kurt E., Mark Aldenderfer, and Karen Doehner
2000 *Working Together: Native Americans and Archaeologists*. Society for American Archaeology, Washington, D.C.

Dongoske, Kurt E., and Roger Anyon
1997 Federal Archaeology: Tribes, Diatribes, and Tribulations. In *Native Americans and Archaeologists: Stepping Stones to Common Ground*. Edited by N. Swidler, K. Dongoske, R. Anyon, and A. Downer, 188–96. AltaMira Press, Walnut Creek, California.

Dongoske, Kurt E., T. J. Ferguson, and Michael Yeatts
1993 Ethics of Field Research for the Hopi Tribe. Paper prepared for the Society for American Archaeology Ethical Issues and Archaeology Workshop, Reno, Nevada.

Dongoske, Kurt E., Michael Yeatts, Roger Anyon, and T. J. Ferguson
1997 Archaeological Cultures and Cultural Affiliation: Hopi and Zuni Perspectives in the American Southwest. *American Antiquity* 62(4):600–8.

Downer, Alan
1997 Archaeologists–Native American Relations. In *Native Americans and Archaeologists: Stepping Stones to Common Ground*. Edited by N. Swidler, K. Dongoske, R. Anyon, and A. Downer, 23–34. AltaMira Press, Walnut Creek, California.

Downey, Roger
2000 *The Riddle of the Bones: Politics. Science, Race and the Story of Kennewick Man*. Copernicus Books, New York.

Doyel, David E.
1982 Medicine Men, Ethnic Significance, and Cultural Resource Management. *American Antiquity* 47(3):634–42.

Durie, Edward T.
1999 Ethics and Values. Electronic version at http://www.kennett.co.nz/law/indigenous/1999/39.html. Last accessed: July 27, 2000.

Dyck, Noel (editor)
1992 Indigenous Peoples and the Nation-state: "Fourth World" Politics in Canada, Australia, and Norway. *Social and Economic Papers* 14, Institute of Social and Economic Research, Memorial University of Newfoundland.

Echo-Hawk, Roger
1997 Forging a New Ancient History for Native America. In *Native Americans and Archaeologists: Stepping Stones to Common Ground.* Edited by N. Swidler, K. Dongoske, R. Anyon, and A. Downer, 88–102. AltaMira Press, Walnut Creek, California.

Everitt, B. S.
1992 *The Analysis of Contingency Tables.* 2nd ed. Monographs on Statistics and Applied Probability, 8. Chapman & Hall, London.

Fagan, Brian M.
1987 *The Great Journey: The Peopling of Ancient America.* Thames and Hudson, London.

Fagan, John L.
1999 Chapter 4: Analysis of Lithic Artifact Embedded in the Columbia Park Remains. In *Report on the Non-destructive Examination, Description, and Analysis of the Human Remains from Columbia Park, Kennewick, Washington.* U.S. Department of the Interior, Washington, D.C.

Ferguson, T. J.
1979 Letter to the author. July 19.

1984 Archaeological Ethics and Values in a Tribal Cultural Resource Management Program at the Pueblo of Zuni. In *Ethics and Values in Archeology.* Edited by E. Green, 224–35. The Free Press, London.

1996 Native Americans and the Practice of Archaeology. *Annual Review of Anthropology* 25:63–79.

Fluehr-Lobban, Carolyn (editor)
1991 *Ethics and the Profession of Anthropology: Dialogue for a New Era.* University of Pennsylvania Press, Philadelphia.

Forbes, Jack D.
1980 *Apache, Navajo, and Spaniard.* University of Oklahoma Press, Norman.

Ford, James A., and Gordon R. Willey
1941 An Interpretation of the Prehistory of the Eastern United States. *American Anthropologist* 43(3):325–63.

Fowler, Donald D.
  1987 Uses of the Past: Archaeology in the Service of the State. *American Antiquity* 52(2):229–48.

Fowler, Floyd J., Jr.
  1984 *Survey Research Methods*. Applied Social Research Methods Series, vol. 1. Sage Publications, Beverly Hills, California.

Fredin, Adeline
  1990 Colville Confederated Tribes. In *Preservation on the Reservation: Native Americans, Native American Lands and Archaeology*. Edited by A. Klesert and A. Downer, 289–99. Navajo Nation Papers in Anthropology Number 26. Navajo Nation Archaeology Department and the Navajo Nation Historic Preservation Department, Windowrock.

Friedman, Milton
  1937 The Use of Ranks to Avoid the Assumption of Normality Implicit in the Analysis of Variance. *Journal of the American Statistical Association* 32:675–701.

Gilles, Karl, and Gerard O'Regan
  1994 Murihiku Resolution of Koiwi Tangata Management. *New Zealand Museum Journal* 24:30–31.

Goldstein, Lynne, and Keith Kintigh
  1990 Ethics and the Reburial Controversy. *American Antiquity* 55(3):585–91.

Gough, Austin
  1996 The New Official Religion and the Retreat of Western Science. *Archaeology in New Zealand* 39:131–38.

Gramly , R. M.
  1990 Archaeological Excavation Permit Application. March 14, 1990.

  1991 Letter to the author. February 23.

Grange, Roger T., Jr.
  1968 Pawnee and Lower Loup Pottery. Nebraska State Historical Society, *Publications in Anthropology*, No. 3.

Green, Ernestine L. (editor)
  1984 *Ethics and Values in Archeology*. The Free Press, London.

Greenberg, Joseph, Christy Turner, and Stephen Zegura
1986 The Settlement of the Americas: A Comparison of the Linguistic, Dental, and Genetic Evidence. *Current Anthropology* 27(5):477–97.

Gummerman, George
1987 The Struggle toward a SOPA Reburial Policy. SOPA *Newsletter* 11(8):1–2.

Gunnerson, James H.
1987 *Archaeology of the High Plains*. Bureau of Land Management, Cultural Resource Series 19, Denver.

Hagey, Jason
1998 Corps Starts to Cover Kennewick Man Site. *Tri-City Herald*, 7 April.

Hall, Louis
1971 Archaeologists and the Indians. *Akwesasne Notes*, 3(6):10. Rooseveltown, New York.

Hamilton, Christopher
1995 A Cautionary Perspective. In *Ethics in American Archaeology: Challenges for the 1990s*. Edited by M. J. Lynott and A. Wylie, 57–63. Society for American Archaeology, Washington, D.C.

Haven, Samuel F.
1856 Archaeology of the United States. *Smithsonian Contributions to Knowledge* 8:1–168. Washington, D.C.

Heritage Conservation and Recreation Services
1978 *Policy on Disposition of Human Remains*. Secretary of the Interior.

Higginbotham, Dean
1982 Native Americans versus Archaeologists: The Legal Issues. *American Indian Law Review* 10:91–115.

Hinsley, Curtis
1983 *Savages and Scientists: The Smithsonian Institution and the Development of American Anthropology, 1846–1910*. Smithsonian Institution Press, Washington, D.C.

Hogan, Anita
1995 Museum Acquisition and Maori Taonga. *Archaeology in New Zealand* 38:271–79.

Holt, H. Barry
1983 A Cultural Resource Management Dilemma: Anasazi Ruins and
the Navajos. *American Antiquity* 48(3):594–99.

Horn, Amanda L.
1997 The Kennewick Man Loses Sleep over NAGPRA: Native Americans and Scientists Wrestle over Cultural Remains. *Sovereignty Symposium X*, 501–24. Oklahoma Bar Association, Oklahoma City.

Hosmer, Charles B., Jr.
1965 *Presence of the Past*. Putnam, New York.

1981 *Preservation Comes of Age: From Williamsburg to the National Trust,
1926–1949*. National Trust Press, Charlottesville.

Hubert, Jane
1994 A Proper Place for the Dead: A Critical Review of the Reburial Issue. In *Conflict in the Archaeology of Living Traditions*. Edited by R.
Layton, 131–66. Routledge, New York.

Huckleberry, Gary, and Julie K. Stein
1999 Chapter 3: Analysis of Sediments Associated with Human Remains
Found at Columbia Park, Kennewick, WA. In *Report on the Non-
destructive Examination, Description, and Analysis of the Human Remains from Columbia Park, Kennewick, Washington*. U.S. Department
of the Interior, Washington, D.C.

Hutt, Sherry
1992 Illegal Trafficking in Native American Human Remains and
Cultural Items: A New Protection Tool. *Arizona State Law Journal*
(24)1:135–50.

Hutt, Sherry, Elwood W. Jones, and Martin E. McAllister
1992 Archaeological Resource Protection. Preservation Press, Washington, D.C.

Jahreskog, Birgitta (editor)
1982 *The Sami National Minority in Sweden*. Rattsfonden (The Legal
Rights Foundation), Amqvist and Wiksell International, Stockholm,
Sweden.

Jelderks, Magistrate John
1997 Opinion, *Bonnichsen* v. *United States*, USDC CV No. 96-1481-JE. Elec-

tronic version at http://www.goonline.com/science/kennewic/
court/opinion.htm. Last accessed: July 27, 2000.

Johnson, Elden
1973 Professional Responsibilities and the American Indian. *American Antiquity* 38(2):129–30.

Jones, D. Gareth, and Robyn J. Harris
1998 Archaeological Human Remains. *Current Anthropology* 39(2):253–64.

Kehoe, Alice Beck
1998 *The Land of Prehistory*. Routledge Press, New York.

King, Thomas F.
1972 Archaeological Law and the American Indian. *The Indian Historian* 5(3):31–35.

1998 *Cultural Resource Laws and Practice: An Introductory Guide*. Heritage Resources Management Series 1, AltaMira Press, Walnut Creek, California.

2000 *Federal Planning and Historic Places: The Section 106 Process*. Heritage Resources Management Series 2, AltaMira Press, Walnut Creek, California.

King, Thomas F., Patricia Parker Hickman, and Gary Berg
1977 *Anthropology in Historic Preservation: Caring for Culture's Clutter*. Academic Press, New York.

Klesert, Anthony L., and Michael J. Andrews
1988 The Treatment of Human Remains on Navajo Lands. *American Antiquity* 53(2):310–20.

Klesert, Anthony L., and Alan S. Downer (editors)
1990 *Preservation on the Reservation: Native Americans, Native American Lands and Archaeology*. Navajo Nation Papers in Anthropology Number 26. Navajo Nation Archaeology Department and the Navajo Nation Historic Preservation Department, Windowrock, Arizona.

Kluckholn, Clyde
1940 The Conceptual Structure in Middle American Studies. In *The Maya and Their Neighbors*. Edited by C. L. Hay et al., 41–51. D. Appleton-Century Company, New York.

Knudson, Ruthann
1991 The Archaeological Public Trust in Context. In *Protecting the Past*. Edited by G. S. Smith and J. E. Ehrenhard, 3–8. CRC Press, Boca Raton, Florida.

Landau, Patricia M., and D. Gentry Steele
1996 Why Anthropologists Study Human Remains. *American Indian Quarterly* 20(2):209–28.

Layton, Robert (editor)
1994 *Conflict in the Archaeology of Living Traditions*. Routledge, New York.

Lee, Mike
1997a Tribes Able to Testify in Kennewick Man Case. *Tri-City Herald*, 3 May.

1997b Senate Revisits Kennewick Man Controversy. *Tri-City Herald*, 16 July.

1997c Doc Pushes Bill to Study Old Bones. *Tri-City Herald*, 14 November.

1997d Researchers Seek Clues at Kennewick Man Site. *Tri-City Herald*, 14 December.

1998a Corps Plans to Cover Kennewick Man Site. *Tri-City Herald*, 3 January.

1998b Senate Steps in to Keep Kennewick Man Site Uncovered. *Tri-City Herald*, 18 March.

1998c Corps Ready to Bury Kennewick Man Site. *Tri-City Herald*, 25 March.

1998d Scientists Say Kennewick Man Bones Treated Poorly. *Tri-City Herald*, 2 July.

1998e Tribes, Asatru Pay Respect to Old Bones before Move to Seattle Museum. *Tri-City Herald*, 30 October.

2000a Experts Chosen to Make Links to Kennewick Man. *Tri-City Herald*, 4 January.

2000b Lab Tests Support Age of Kennewick Man. *Tri-City Herald*, 13 January.

2000c DNA Testing in Works for Bones. *Tri-City Herald*, 1 February.

2000d Tribes Criticize Plan to Test DNA of Old Bones. *Tri-City Herald*, 2 February.

Levy, Janet
1995 Ethics Code of the American Anthropological Association and Its Relevance for SAA. In *Ethics in American Archaeology: Challenges for the 1990s*. Edited by M. J. Lynott and A. Wylie, 86–93. Society for American Archaeology, Washington, D.C.

Lewins, Frank
1991 Theoretical and Political Implications of the Dynamic Approach to Aboriginality. In Reconsidering Aboriginality. *Australian Journal of Anthropology*, Special Issue 2. Edited by S. Thiele, 171–78. Anthropological Society of New South Wales, Sydney.

Lurie, Nancy Oestreich
1988 Relations between Indians and Anthropologists. In *History of Indian-white Relations*. Edited by W. Washburn, 548–56, Handbook of North American Indians, vol. 4. Smithsonian Institution Press, Washington, D.C.

Lynott, Mark J.
1997 Ethical Principles and Archaeological Practice: Development of an Ethics Policy. *American Antiquity* 62(4):589–99.

Lynott, Mark, and Alison Wylie
1993 *Ethical Issues and Archaeology*. NSF Conference Grant Proposal.

1995 *Ethics in American Archaeology: Challenges for the 1990s*. Society for American Archaeology, Special Report.

Maddock, Kenneth
1991 Metamorphosing the Sacred in Australia. In Reconsidering Aboriginality. *Australian Journal of Anthropology*, Special Issue 2. Edited by S. Thiele, 213–32. Anthropological Society of New South Wales, Sydney.

Martin, Rena
1997 How Traditional Navajos View Historic Preservation: A Question of Interpretation. In *Native Americans and Archaeologists: Stepping Stones to Common Ground*. Edited by N. Swidler, K. Dongoske, R. Anyon, and A. Downer, 128–34. AltaMira Press, Walnut Creek, California.

McBride, Delbert J.
1971 The Ethics of Ethnic Collections. *Western Museums Quarterly* 8(1):10–12.

McGimsey, Charles R., and Hester A. Davis (editors)
1977 *The Management of Archaeological Resources: The Airlie House Report.* Special Publication of the Society for American Archaeology.

McGregor, John C.
1941 *Southwestern Archaeology.* John Wiley and Sons, New York.

McGuire, Randall H.
1992a Archaeology and the First Americans. *American Anthropologist* 94(4):816–36.

1992b *A Marxist Archaeology.* Academic Press, San Diego.

1997 Why Have Archaeologists Thought the Real Indians Were Dead and What Can We Do About It? In *Indians and Anthropologists: Vine Deloria Jr., and the Critique of Anthropology.* Edited by T. Biolsi and L. Zimmerman, 63–91. University of Arizona Press, Tucson.

McManamom, Francis P.
1997 Letter to Lieutenant Colonel Donald J. Curtis. December 23.

1999 Chapter 1: The Initial Scientific Examination, Description, and Analysis of the Kennewick Man Human Remains. In *Report on the Non-destructive Examination, Description, and Analysis of the Human Remains from Columbia Park, Kennewick, Washington.* U.S. Department of the Interior, Washington, D.C.

Meehan, B.
1984 Aboriginal Skeletal Remains. *Australian Archaeology* 19:122–47.

Mehringer, Peter J., Jr.
1988 Clovis Cache Found: Weapons of Ancient Americans. *National Geographic* 174(4):500–3.

1989 *Age of the Clovis Cache at East Wenatchee, Washington.* Report presented to the Washington State Historic Preservation Office, Pullman.

Mehringer, Peter J., Jr., and F. F. Foit
1990 Volcanic Ash Dating of the Clovis Cache at East Wenatchee, Washington. *National Geographic Research* 6(4):495–503.

Mehringer, Peter J., J. C. Sheppard, and F. F. Foit
1984 The Age of Glacier Peak Tephra in West-central Montana. *Quaternary Research* 21(1):36–41.

Meighan, Clement
1984 Archeology: Science or Sacrilege? In *Ethics and Values in Archeology.* Edited by E. Green, 208–23. The Free Press, London.

1992 Some Scholars' Views on Reburial. *American Antiquity* 57:704–10.

Meltzer, David J.
1983 The Antiquity of Man and the Development of American Archaeology. In *Advances in Archaeological Method and Theory,* vol. 6. Edited by M. Schiffer, 1–51. Academic Press, New York.

1985 North American Archaeology and Archaeologists, 1879–1934. *American Antiquity* 50:249–60.

1989 Why Don't We Know When the First People Came to North America? *American Antiquity* 54(3):471–90.

Meltzer, David J., Donald K. Grayson, Geraldo Ardila, Alex W. Barker, Dena F. Dincauze, C. Vance Haynes, Francisco Mena, Laurtaro Nunez, and Dennis J. Stanford
1997 On the Pleistocene Antiquity of Monte Verde, Southern Chile. *American Antiquity* 62(4):659–63.

Messenger, Phyllis Mauch (editor)
1989 *The Ethics of Collecting Cultural Property: Whose Culture? Whose Property?* University of New Mexico Press, Albuquerque.

Mills, Barbara J., and T. J. Ferguson
1998 Preservation and Research of Sacred Sites by the Zuni Indian Tribe of New Mexico. *Human Organization* 57(1):30–42.

Minthorn, Armand
1996 Human Remains Should Be Reburied. Electronic version at http://www.umatilla.nsn.us/kennman.html. Last accessed: July 27, 2000.

Monger, E.
1970 A Preliminary Report of the Larned Site. *Kansas Anthropological Association, Newsletter* 15(8):1–15.

Morse, Brad
  1997 Comparative Assessments of Indigenous Peoples in Australasia,
  Scandinavia, and North America. *Sovereignty Symposium X*, 309–44.
  Oklahoma Bar Association, Oklahoma City.

Mulk, Inga-Maria
  1997 Sacrificial Places and Their Meaning in Sami Society. In *Sacred Sites,
  Sacred Places*. Edited by D. Carmichael, J. Hubert, B. Reeves, and
  A. Schande, 121–31. Routledge, New York.

Mulvaney, John
  1991 Past Regained, Future Lost: The Kow Swamp Pleistocene Burials.
  Antiquity 65:12–21.

Mulvaney, John, and Johan Kamminga
  1999 *Prehistory of Australia*. Smithsonian Institution Press, Washington,
  D.C.

Murray, Tim
  1996 Coming to Terms with the Living: Some Aspects of Repatriation
  for the Archaeologist. *Antiquity* 70:217–20.

Nason, James D.
  1971 Museums and American Indians: An Inquiry into Relationships.
  Western Museums Quarterly 8(1):13–17.

National Park Service
  1996 National Historic Preservation Program Expanded: Twelve Tribes
  Welcomed as Full Participants in the National Historic Preservation Program. Electronic version at http://www2.cr.nps.gov/
  tribal/thpo1.htm. Last accessed: July 26, 2000.

New Zealand
  1840 *Treaty of Waitangi*. Electronic version at http://www.govt.nz/
  aboutnz/treaty.hph3. Last accessed: July 27, 2000.

Nicholas, George P., and Thomas D. Andrews (editors)
  1997 *At a Crossroads: Archaeology and First Peoples in Canada*. Archaeology Press, Department of Archaeology, Simon Frazier University,
  Burnaby, British Columbia.

Nichols, Deborah L., Anthony L. Klesert, and Roger Anyon
  1989 Ancestral Sites, Shrines, and Graves: Native American Perspectives

on the Ethics of Collecting Cultural Properties. In *The Ethics of Collecting Cultural Property: Whose Culture? Whose Property?* Edited by P. M. Messenger, 27–38. University of New Mexico Press, Albuquerque.

Nicholson, Bev, David Pokotylo, and Ron Williamson
1996 *Statement of Principles for Ethical Conduct Pertaining to Aboriginal Peoples: A Report from the Aboriginal Heritage Committee.* Jointly sponsored by the Canadian Archaeological Association and the Department of Canadian Heritage.

Niquette, Charles M.
1987 A Proposed SOPA Policy on the Treatment of Human Remains. SOPA *Newsletter* 11(4):1–2.

Nosanchuk, T. A.
1972 The Vignette as an Experimental Approach to the Study of Social Status: An Exploratory Study. *Social Science Research* 1:107–20.

O'Hagan, Maureen
1998 Bones of Contention: The Agendas That Have Brought a 9,300-Year-Old Skeleton to Life. *Willamette Week*, 22 April. Electronic version at http://www.wweek.com/html/cover042298.html. Last accessed: July 27, 2000.

Olsson, Sven E., and Dave Lewis
1995 Welfare Rules and Indigenous Rights: The Sami People and the Nordic Welfare States. In *Social Welfare with Indigenous Peoples.* Edited by J. Dixon and R. P. Scheurell, 141–85. Routledge Press, New York and London.

Ortiz, Alfonso
1972 An Indian Anthropologist's Perspective on Anthropology. In *The American Indian Reader: Anthropology.* Edited by J. Henry, 6–12. Indian Historian Press, San Francisco.

Pardoe, Colin
1992 Arches of Radii, Corridors of Power: Reflections on Current Archaeological Practice. In *Power, Knowledge, and Aborigines.* Edited by B. Attwood and J. Arnold, 132–41. La Trobe University Press, Bundoora, Victoria.

Peregoy, Robert M.
	1992 The Legal Basis, Legislative History, and Implementation of Nebraska's Landmark Reburial Legislation. *Arizona State Law Journal* 24(1):329–89.

Petit, Charles
	1998 Rediscovering America. *U.S. News & World Report*, 12 October, 56–64.

Powell, Joseph, and Jerome C. Rose
	1999 Chapter 2: Report on the Osteological Assessment of the "Kennewick Man" Skeleton (CENWW.97.Kennewick). In *Report on the Non-destructive Examination, Description, and Analysis of the Human Remains from Columbia Park, Kennewick, Washington.* U.S. Department of the Interior, Washington, D.C.

Preston, Douglas
	1997 The Lost Man. *The New Yorker*, 16 June, 70–81.

Pullar, Gordon
	1994 The Qikertatmiut and the Scientist: Fifty Years of Clashing World Views. In *Reckoning with the Dead: The Larsen Bay Repatriation and the Smithsonian Institution.* Edited by T. L. Bray and T. W. Killion, 15–25. Smithsonian Press, Washington, D.C.

Quick, Polly (editor)
	1985 *Proceedings of the Reburial Conference.* Society for American Archaeology.

Ravesloot, John C.
	1997 Changing Native American Perceptions of Archaeology and Archaeologists. In *Native Americans and Archaeologists: Stepping Stones to Common Ground.* Edited by N. Swidler, K. Dongoske, R. Anyon, and A. Downer, 172–77. AltaMira Press, Walnut Creek, California.

Riding In, James
	1992 Without Ethics and Morality: A Historical Overview of Imperial Archaeology and American Indians. *Arizona State Law Journal* (24)1:11–34.

Ritchie, William A.
	1938 A Perspective of Northeastern Archaeology. *American Antiquity* 4(2):94–112.

Rose, Jerome C., Thomas J. Green, and Victoria D. Green
1996 NAGPRA Is Forever: The Future of Osteology and the Repatriation of Skeletons. *Annual Review of Anthropology* 25: 81–103.

Rosen, Lawrence
1980 The Excavation of American Indian Burial Sites: A Problem in Law and Professional Responsibility. *American Anthropologist* 82(1):5–27.

Rosenswig, Robert M.
1997 Ethics in Canadian Archaeology: An International, Comparative Analysis. *Journal Canadien d'Archeologie* 21:99–114.

Roughly, Alan R.
1991 Racism, Aboriginality, and Textuality: Toward a Deconstructing Discourse. In Reconsidering Aboriginality. *Australian Journal of Anthropology,* Special Issue 2. Edited by S. Thiele, 202–12. Anthropological Society of New South Wales, Sydney.

Ruby, Robert H., and John A. Brown
1986 *A Guide to the Indians of the Pacific Northwest.* University of Oklahoma Press, Norman.

Ruong, Israel
1982 Sami Usage and Customs. In *The Sami National Minority in Sweden.* Edited by B. Jahreskog, 23–35. Rattsfonden (The Legal Rights Foundation), Amqvist and Wiksell International, Stockholm, Sweden.

Sackett, Lee
1991 Promoting Primitivism: Conservationist Depictions of Aboriginal Australians. In Reconsidering Aboriginality. *Australian Journal of Anthropology,* Special Issue 2. Edited by S. Thiele, 233–46. Anthropological Society of New South Wales, Sydney.

Sampson, Don
1997 (Former) Tribal Chair Questions Scientists' Motives and Credibility. Electronic version at http://www.umatilla.nsn.us/kennman2.html. Last accessed: July 27, 2000.

Schafer, Dave
1996 Skull Likely Early White Settler. *Tri-City Herald,* 30 July.

Schmid, Calvin F.
1966 Basic Statistical Concepts and Techniques. In *Scientific Social Surveys and Research.* Edited by P. V. Young, 274–347. Prentice Hall, Englewood Cliffs, New Jersey.

Schoolcraft, Henry R.
1854 *Historical and Statistical Information Respecting the History, Condition, and Prospects of the Indian Tribes of the United States, Part IV.* Lippincott, Grambo, Philadelphia.

Shutler, Richard, Jr. (editor)
1983 *Early Man in the New World.* Sage, Beverly Hills, California.

Slayman, Andrew
1997 A Battle over Bones. *Archaeology* 50(1):16–23.

Smith, George S., and John E. Ehrenhard (editors)
1991 *Protecting the Past.* CRC Press, Boca Raton, Florida.

Society for American Archaeology
1977 By-laws of the Society for American Archaeology. *American Antiquity* 42(2):308–12.

1986 Statement Concerning the Treatment of Human Remains. *Bulletin of the Society for American Archaeology* 4(3):7–8.

1989 Nebraska Passes Reburial Law. *Bulletin of the Society for American Archaeology* 7(5):1–2.

Society of Professional Archaeologists
1976 Code of Ethics, Standards of Research Performance and Institutional Standards. As reprinted in *Ethics and the Profession of Anthropology: Dialogue for a New Era:* appendix E. Edited by C. Fluehr-Lobban, 257–62. University of Pennsylvania Press, Philadelphia.

1986 NCAI Speaks to Reburial Issues. SOPA *Newsletter* 11(1):3.

1990 Zuni Tribal Council Resolution on Reburial. SOPA *Newsletter* 14(3):2.

Sorenson, Eric
1999a B.C.'s "Long Ago Man": A Snapshot in Time. *Seattle Times,* 14 September. Electronic version at http://archives.seattletimes.nwsource.com. Last accessed: July 27, 2000.

1999b B.C. Iceman Found to Be Too "Young" to Affect Settlement Theories. *Seattle Times*, 29 September. Electronic version at http://archives.seattletimes.nwsource.com. Last accessed: July 27, 2000.

Sprague, Roderick
1974 American Indians and American Archaeology. *American Antiquity* 39(1):1–2.

Sprague, Roderick, and Walter W. Birkby
1970 Miscellaneous Columbia Plateau Burials. *Tebiwa* 13(1):1–32.

Stang, John
1996 Many Claim to Have Connection to Kennewick Man. *Tri-City Herald*, 20 December.

Stein, Martin
1989 The Salina Indian Burial Pit Was Long a Tourist Attraction. *Historic Preservation, Newsletter of the Historic Preservation Department* 11(6):4–5. Kansas State Historical Society, Topeka.

Stevenson, Katherine
1998 Testimony June 10, 1998, on HR 2893, a Bill to Amend the Native American Graves Protection and Repatriation Act. Electronic version at http://www.kennewick-man.com/documents/testimony/index.html. Last accessed: July 27, 2000.

Steward, Julian H., and Frank M. Setzler
1938 Function and Configuration in Archaeology. *American Antiquity* 4(1):4–10.

Stoffle, Richard W., and Michael J. Evans
1990 Holistic Conservation and Cultural Triage: American Indian Perspectives on Cultural Resources. *Human Organization* 49(2):91–99.

Stolfus, Alan
1988 Indian Burial Pit Safe from State, for Now. *Salina Journal*, 27 February.

Strong, W. D.
1935 *An Introduction to Nebraska Archaeology*. Smithsonian Miscellaneous Collections 93(10), Washington, D.C.

1940 From History to Prehistory in the Northern Great Plains. In *Essays in Historical Anthropology of North America.* Smithsonian Miscellaneous Collections 100:353–94, Washington, D.C.

Suagee, Dean B.
1982 American Indian Religious Freedom and Cultural Resources Management: Protecting Mother Earth's Caretakers. *American Indian Law Review* 10(1):1–58.

Superintendent of Documents
1996 Native American Graves Protection and Repatriation Act: Hearing before the Committee on Indian Affairs, United States Senate, One Hundred Fourth Congress, First Session, an Oversight Hearing on Public Law 101-601, to Provide the Authority and Mechanism for the Repatriation of Native American Human Remains, Funerary Objects, Sacred Objects, and Objects of Cultural Patrimony. December 6, 1995. Washington, D.C.

1999 Native American Graves Protection and Repatriation Act: Hearing before the Committee on Indian Affairs, United States Senate, One Hundred Sixth Congress, First Session on Public Law 101-601, to Provide for the Protection of Native American Graves. April 20, 1999, Washington, D.C.

Swidler, Nina, Kurt Dongoske, Roger Anyon, and Alan Downer (editors)
1997 *Native Americans and Archaeologists: Stepping Stones to Common Ground.* AltaMira Press, Walnut Creek, California.

Talmage, Valerie
1982 The Violation of Sepulture: Is It Legal to Excavate Human Burials? *Archaeology* 35(6):44–49.

Thiele, Steven (editor)
1991a Reconsidering Aboriginality. *The Australian Journal of Anthropology,* Special Issue 2. Anthropological Society of New South Wales, Sydney.

1991b Taking a Sociological Approach to Europeanness (Whiteness) and Aboriginality (Blackness). In Reconsidering Aboriginality. *Australian Journal of Anthropology,* Special Issue 2. Edited by S. Thiele, 179–201. Anthropological Society of New South Wales, Sydney.

Thies, Randall M.
1999 Letter to the author. December 14.

Thomas, David Hurst
  2000 *Skull Wars: Archaeology and the Search for Native American Identity.*
  Basic Books, New York.

Trigger, Bruce
  1980 Archaeology and the Image of the American Indian. *American Antiquity* 45(4):662–76.

  1986 Prehistoric Archaeology and American Society: An Historical Perspective. In *American Archaeology Past and Future.* Edited by D. J. Meltzer, D. D. Fowler, and J. A. Sabloff, 187–215. Smithsonian Institution Press, Washington, D.C.

  1989 *A History of Archaeological Thought.* Cambridge University Press, Cambridge.

Trope, Jack F., and Walter Echo-Hawk
  1992 The Native American Graves Protection and Repatriation Act: Background and Legislative History. *Arizona State Law Journal* (24)1:35–77.

Tsosie, Rebecca
  1997 Indigenous Rights and Archaeology. In *Native Americans and Archaeologists: Stepping Stones to Common Ground.* Edited by N. Swidler, K. Dongoske, R. Anyon, and A. Downer, 64–76. AltaMira Press, Walnut Creek, California.

TwoBears, Davina
  2000 A Navajo Student's Perception: Anthropology and the Navajo Nation Archaeology Department Student Training Program. In *Working Together: Native Americans and Archaeologists.* Edited by K. E. Dongoske, M. Aldenderfer, and K. Doehner, 15–22. Society for American Archaeology, Washington, D.C.

Ubelaker, Douglas H., and Lauryn Guttenplan Grant
  1989 Human Skeletal Remains: Preservation or Reburial? *Yearbook of Physical Anthropology* 32:249–87.

Ucko, Peter
  1994 Foreword. In *Archaeology in the Conflict of Living Traditions.* Edited by R. Layton, ix–xvii. Routledge, New York.

Verrengia, Joseph
  1999 Iceman Could Shed Light on First Americans. *Seattle Times*, 26 August.

Electronic version at http://archives.seattletimes.nwsource.com. Last accessed: July 27, 2000.

Waitt, R. B., and B. F. Atwater
1989 Stratigraphic and Geomorphic Evidence for Dozens of Last-glacial Floods. In *Glacial Lake Missoula and the Channeled Scabland*, 28th International Geological Congress Field Trip Guidebook T310. Edited by R. M. Breckenridge, 37–50. American Geophysical Union, Washington, D.C.

Waldorf, D. C.
1991a Finding the Pony. In *CHIPS, A Publication of Flint Knappers' Guild International* 3(1):2–4.

1991b The Ritchey Cache: Some Observations. In *CHIPS, A Publication of Flint Knappers' Guild International* 3(1):4–7.

Warren, Karen J.
1989 A Philosophical Perspective on the Ethics and Resolution of Cultural Properties Issues. In *The Ethics of Collecting Cultural Property: Whose Culture? Whose Property?* Edited by P. M. Messenger, 1–25. University of New Mexico Press, Albuquerque.

Watkins, Joe
1980 Memorandum to the Departmental Consulting Archaeologist Re: The HCRS/IAS "Policy for the Disposition of Human Remains." On file with author.

1994 *Ethics and Culture Conflicts: An Examination of Archaeologists' Responses to Questionnaire Scenarios Concerning the Relationship between American Indians and Archaeologists.* Unpublished Ph.D. dissertation, Southern Methodist University.

1995 Committee on Native American Relations. *SAA Bulletin* 13(4):14–15.

1999 Native American Archaeology or Archaeology of Native Americans? Public Policy and Native Americans: How Do We Go From Here? Public Policy Panel, Clovis and Beyond Conference, Santa Fe.

2000 A Native American Perspective: The Power of Respect. *Scientific American's Discovering Archaeology* 2(1):68–69.

Watkins, Joe, K. Anne Pyburn, and Pam Cressey
2000 Community Relations: What the Practicing Archaeologist Needs

to Know to Work Effectively with Local and/or Descendant Communities. In *Teaching Archaeology in the Twenty-first Century*. Edited by S. J. Bender and G. Smith, 73–81. Society for American Archaeology, Washington, D.C.

Watson, Patty Jo (editor)
1986 Announcement of Plenary Session. SAA Annual Meeting, New Orleans, April 24, 1986. *Bulletin of the Society for American Archaeology* 4(1):1.

Wedel, Waldo R.
1936 *An Introduction to Pawnee Archaeology*. Bureau of American Ethnology, Bulletin 112, Washington, D. C.

1938 *The Direct Historical Approach to Pawnee Archaeology*. Smithsonian Miscellaneous Collections 97(7). Washington, D.C.

1959 *An Introduction to Kansas Archaeology*. Bureau of American Ethnology, Bulletin 174, Washington, D.C.

1961 *Prehistoric Man on the Great Plains*. University of Oklahoma Press, Norman.

Welsh, Peter H.
1992 Repatriation and Cultural Preservation: Potent Objects, Potent Pasts. *University of Michigan Journal of Law Reform* 25(3/4):837–65.

Wendorf, Fred, Nancy Fox, and Orian L. Lewis
1956 *Pipeline Archaeology: Reports of Salvage Operations in the Southwest on El Paso Natural Gas Company Projects 1950–1953*. Published Jointly by the Laboratory of Anthropology and the Museum of Northern Arizona, Santa Fe and Flagstaff.

Wheat, Dan
1990a Archaeologist Calls for Clovis Dig Moratorium. *Wenatchee World*, 14 October.

1990b WSU Scientist Refused to Join. *Wenatchee World*, 14 October.

1990c Gramley Defends His Sales of Artifacts. *Wenatchee World*, 14 October.

1990d Landowner Fed Up with Dig Squabbles. *Wenatchee World*, 18 October.

1990e Cache Has Potential for Human Remains. *Wenatchee World*, 23 October.

1990f Clovis Pit Edges Defined; Habitation Debated. *Wenatchee World*, 9 November.

1990g Archaeologists Annoyed with Dig Director. *Wenatchee World*, 12 November.

1990h Clovis Cache May Be Planted over. *Wenatchee World*, 20 November.

1991a Several Groups Explore Clovis Site Purchase. *Wenatchee World*, 29 April.

1991b Buffalo Museum Offers $485,000. *Wenatchee World*, 29 April.

1991c Archaeologists, Tribe Set Forth Dig Principles. *Wenatchee World*, 1 May.

1991d Bones May Be Sled Runners. *Wenatchee World*, 1 May.

1991e Colvilles to Be Consulted on Digs in Future. *Wenatchee World*, 2 May.

1991f Ethics Could Be Part of Permit Process. *Wenatchee World*, 6 May.

1991g Gramly Applauds Clovis Purchase. *Wenatchee World*, 1 August.

Willey, Gordon R., and Jeremy Sabloff
1980 *A History of American Archaeology*. 2nd ed. W. H. Freeman and Co., New York.

Wilson, Paul E., and Elaine Oser Zingg
1974 What is America's Heritage? Historic Preservation and American Indian Culture. *Kansas Law Review* 22(3):413–53.

Winter, Joseph C.
1980 Indian Heritage Preservation and Archaeologists. *American Antiquity* 45(1):121–31.

1984 The Way to Somewhere: Ethics in American Archaeology. In *Ethics and Values in Archeology*. Edited by E. Green, 36–47. The Free Press, London.

Witty, Thomas A.
1989a Comments on Proposed Burial Legislation. *Journal of the Kansas Anthropological Association* 9(7):124–35.

1989b New Law to Protect Unmarked Burial Sites in Kansas. *Historic*

Preservation, Newsletter of the Historic Preservation Department 11(6):3. Kansas State Historical Society, Topeka.

1990 The Reburial Issue Comes to Kansas: The Closing of the Indian Burial Pit at Salina. Paper presented at the 48th Meeting of the Plains Anthropological Society, Oklahoma City.

Wren, Patricia
1990a Tribes Want Clovis Dig Stopped. *Wenatchee World*, 20 July.

1990b Archaeologist Defends Record Despite Critics' Doubts. *Wenatchee World*, 20 July.

Wright, Karen
1999 First Americans. *Discover*, February, 53–63.

Wyman, Leland C.
1983 Navajo Ceremonial System. In *Southwest.* Edited by A. Ortiz, 536–57. Handbook of North American Indians, vol. 10. Smithsonian Institution, Washington, D.C.

Young, Pauline V.
1966 *Scientific Social Surveys and Research.* 4th ed. Prentice Hall, Englewood Cliffs, New Jersey.

Zeder, Melinda
1997 *The American Archaeologist: A Profile.* AltaMira Press, Walnut Creek, California.

Zier, Lillian
1989a Artifacts to Be Returned to Burial Pit. *Salina Journal*, 13 July.

1989b Indian Burial Pit Closed; State to Take over Tuesday. *Salina Journal*, 29 December.

Zimmerman, Larry
1995 Regaining Our Nerve: Ethics, Values, and the Transformation of Archaeology. In *Ethics in American Archaeology: Challenges for the 1990s.* Edited by M. J. Lynott and A. Wylie, 64–67. Society for American Archaeology, Washington, D.C.

1997 Anthropology and Responses to the Reburial Issue. In *Indians and Anthropologists: Vine Deloria Jr., and the Critique of Anthropology.*

Edited by T. Biolsi and L. Zimmerman, 92–112. University of Arizona Press, Tucson.

Zimmerman, Larry, and Leonard R. Bruguier
1994 Indigenous Peoples and the World Archaeological Congress Code of Ethics. *Public Archaeology Review* 2(1):5–8. Indiana University-Purdue University, Indianapolis.

Index

~o⋈o~

About the Author

Joe Watkins, born at Talihina Indian Hospital in 1951, is half Choctaw Indian by blood. His early childhood experiences with his Choctaw grandmother in southeastern Oklahoma greatly influenced his desire to learn more about his tribe's history and his Choctaw heritage, and has also allowed him to bring a unique perspective into the field of archaeology. He has been involved in archaeology for more than thirty years, receiving his Bachelor's of Arts in anthropology in 1973 from the University of Oklahoma and his Master's of Arts in anthropology from Southern Methodist University in 1977. His doctorate from Southern Methodist University in 1994 focused on archaeologists' responses to questionnaire scenarios concerning the relationship between American Indians and archaeologists.

His work in various facets of cultural resource management—as a land manager and as a private consultant, as a federal employee and as a state employee, and as an archaeologist and an American Indian—has exposed him to all of the roles of the federal cultural resources management system. Currently employed as the Anadarko Agency Archeologist for the Bureau of Indian Affairs in southwest Oklahoma, he has developed consultation procedures with the tribes that make up the agency jurisdiction to include education and training on cultural resources management, preservation laws and procedures, and technical assistance regarding cultural,

NAGPRA, environmental, and heritage issues. He is a research associate in the Department of Anthropology and the Mathers Museum at Indiana University in Bloomington, where his research interests include aboriginal populations/archaeologist relations, ethics in archaeology, archaeology of the southern Great Plains, archaeology in the public interest, the study of archaeology, and public archaeology/cultural resource management.